Amazon

Taking a political economy of media approach, this book examines Amazon as a significant actor in the global media landscape. Amazon is mainly conceived in the popular consciousness and media commentary as a corporate body, selling products and services to individual consumers and organisations, but Brevini and Swiatek show that Amazon has become a communication giant that trades in diversified media (its own and others) and exerts a significant influence on global communication, especially through its online services. Further, the authors provide evidence of Amazon's multiple influences on politics, economics, and culture.

With its comprehensive and critical overview, this book is ideal for students, scholars, and researchers of media and communication studies and political economy.

Benedetta Brevini is Associate Professor in Communication and Media, specialising in political economy of communication, at the University of Sydney, Australia. She writes on *The Guardian*'s Comment is Free and contributes to a number of print and web publications, including Index of Censorship, openDemocracy, and the Conversation. She is the author of *Public Service Broadcasting Online* (2013) and editor of the volume *Beyond Wikileaks* (2013). Her latest volumes are *Carbon Capitalism and Communication: Confronting Climate Crisis* (2017) and *Climate Change and the Media* (2018). She is currently writing a new book on Artificial Intelligence.

Lukasz Swiatek lectures in media and communications at the University of New South Wales (UNSW) in Sydney, Australia. He has taught a range of undergraduate and postgraduate courses (both junior and senior) in media studies, communication, and international and global studies across universities in Australia and Aotearoa New Zealand. Previously, he worked in publishing and news (as a reporter and editor), as well as integrated communication, in both the corporate and not-for-profit sectors.

Global Media Giants
Series editors: Benjamin J. Birkinbine, Rodrigo Gomez and Janet Wasko

Since the second half of the 20th century, the significance of media corporate power has been increasing in different and complex ways around the world; the power of these companies in political, symbolic and economic terms has been a global issue and concern. In the 21st century, understanding media corporations is essential to understanding the political, economic and socio-cultural dimensions of our contemporary societies.

The **Global Media Giants** series continues the work that began in the series editors' book *Global Media Giants*, providing detailed examinations of the largest and most powerful media corporations in the world.

Alphabet
The Becoming of Google
Micky Lee

Tencent
The Political Economy of China's Surging Internet Giant
Min Tang

Grupo Prisa
Media Power in Contemporary Spain
Luis A. Albornoz, Ana I. Segovia, and Núria Almiron

Amazon
Understanding a Global Communication Giant
Benedetta Brevini and Lukasz Swiatek

For more information about this series, please visit: www.routledge.com/ Global-Media-Giants/book-series/GMG

Amazon
Understanding a Global Communication Giant

**Benedetta Brevini and
Lukasz Swiatek**

NEW YORK AND LONDON

First published 2021
by Routledge
52 Vanderbilt Avenue, New York, NY 10017

and by Routledge
2 Park Square, Milton Park, Abingdon, Oxon, OX14 4RN

Routledge is an imprint of the Taylor & Francis Group, an informa business

© 2021 Taylor & Francis

The right of Benedetta Brevini and Lukasz Swiatek to be identified
as authors of this work has been asserted by them in accordance
with sections 77 and 78 of the Copyright, Designs and Patents Act
1988.

All rights reserved. No part of this book may be reprinted
or reproduced or utilised in any form or by any electronic,
mechanical, or other means, now known or hereafter invented,
including photocopying and recording, or in any information
storage or retrieval system, without permission in writing from the
publishers.

Trademark notice: Product or corporate names may be trademarks
or registered trademarks, and are used only for identification and
explanation without intent to infringe.

Library of Congress Cataloging-in-Publication Data
A catalog record for this book has been requested

ISBN: 978-0-367-36433-5 (hbk)
ISBN: 978-0-367-81671-1 (ebk)

Typeset in Times New Roman
by Apex CoVantage, LLC

This book is dedicated to my Zia. I know you are plotting a lasagne book launch somewhere in the clouds.

Contents

List of Illustrations		viii
Acknowledgements		ix
1	**Introduction**	1
	BENEDETTA BREVINI	
2	**Economic Profile**	7
	BENEDETTA BREVINI	
3	**Political Profile**	22
	BENEDETTA BREVINI AND LUKASZ SWIATEK	
4	**Cultural Profile**	48
	LUKASZ SWIATEK	
5	**Conclusion**	65
	BENEDETTA BREVINI	
	Index	71

Illustrations

Figures

2.1	Revenue Net Income Total Assets: 2004–2019	8

Tables

2.1	Consolidated Statements	9
2.2	Net Sales of the Three Divisions and AWS Sales	10
2.3	Operating Income (Profits) Three Business Divisions: Amazon	10
2.4	Net Sales by Group of Similar Products and Services	11
3.1	Beneficial Owners of Shares: Amazon Shareholders of March 2020	23
3.2	Current Board of Directors, Amazon	24
3.3	The Digital Giants' Spending on Lobbying in the U.S. in 2019	34
3.4	Race and Ethnicity Among Amazon's U.S. Managers and Non-managerial Employees	38

Acknowledgements

Many thanks to our editors—Ben, Janet and Rodrigo—for their very helpful feedback on the early draft. Thank you Emma at Routledge for your support and enthusiasm for the book, before and during the pandemic. Thank you also Edward, for your research assistance and the wonderful conversations on Amazon's latest acquisitions.

1 Introduction

Benedetta Brevini

As I write this introduction, the coronavirus global pandemic is impacting global economies in unforeseen ways. It is not surprising that Amazon, one of the wealthiest corporations in the world, is making the daily news during the coronavirus emergency. When the world as we knew it stopped and lock-downs kicked in, stressed and bored consumers rushed to Amazon to secure precious and not-so-precious commodities without leaving home. The pandemic – and the associated growth of Amazon – has reignited concerns that have been repeatedly raised in the past: Amazon is too big, too powerful, and is insufficiently attentive to its workers.

At the start of the COVID-19 crisis, Amazon CEO Jeff Bezos was asked to explain why a $25 million U.S. relief fund[1] he established to help his own contract employees during the pandemic was also soliciting contributions from the public. Why, the media asked, was the wealthiest man in the world,[2] at the helm of a $1 trillion company, seeking voluntary donations to help its employees?

This was not the only criticism directed at Amazon related to the company's treatment of its employees, who, because of their workplace, are heavily exposed to the risk of contracting COVID-19. Although Amazon refers to its warehouse and delivery workers as "heroes fighting for their communities",[3] performing the crucial work of delivering supplies to locked-down consumers, many of these employees are anxious about the safety of their health. Their options in the face of the pandemic are limited: they can take unpaid time off with no salary at all, or those who test positive for the disease are entitled to two weeks of paid sick leave. As a result, most employees continued to go to work. Many workers have now added a badge to their profiles, stating, "I can't stay home, I work at Amazon".

The pandemic has also highlighted ongoing global issues of wealth inequality, and the impressive rise of Amazon stocks on the NYSE did not go unnoticed. In April 2020 Amazon stocks hit a new record, closing at $2.283

2 Benedetta Brevini

per share, an increase of over 20% in the first quarter. This occurred just as the Standard and Poor (S&P) 500, severely hit by the crisis, lost about 15% of its value. Bezos's net worth increased by nearly $36 billion between March and June 2020, at the peak of the coronavirus crisis, while millions of workers lost their jobs. As Senator Bernie Sanders keeps repeating, "Our society cannot sustain itself when so few have so much, while so many have so little".

Enthusiasts of globalisation argued for years that we had created an interconnected financial system that was resilient enough to help us through major crises. However, the coronavirus crisis, just as the global financial crisis of 2008 before it, has highlighted once again in striking terms that *super capitalism*[4] has failed. From every corner of the world, we turn to public support and public resources to overcome the crisis. Once again, we have had to be rescued by the nation state and especially by centralised banks, charged by government to carry out major plans that are consistent with the social democratic ideals of a welfare state.

In such dire circumstances, with unemployment levels rising, Amazon is still prospering.

Looking at the performance of Amazon in the last weeks of April 2020, coronavirus has offered major opportunities: the company hired 175,000 full- and part-time workers, its online shopping branch kept thriving, as well as its technological and communication branch, with cloud computing and video streaming increasing their demand. Amazon Prime Video is ranked only behind Netflix Inc in popularity in the U.S.

Moreover, during the first three months of 2020, Amazon's shares rose 6%, so that the growth from the beginning of 2020 reached 11%, when S&P 500 was down 15%.

Reflecting on these numbers, one might think that this is the perfect example of the shock doctrine thesis by Naomi Klein,[5] author of the 2007 book *The Shock Doctrine: The Rise of Disaster Capitalism*. In this book, Ms Klein describes disaster capitalism as

> the way in which private industries spring up to directly profit from large-scale crises. . . . We are seeing a very selective use of emergency measures, of the utilization and the instrumentalization and the weaponization of states of emergency to offload risks onto individual workers and families, while the people who are already most cushioned are getting these no-strings-attached bailouts.

As the political economy of communication (PEC)[6] has long shown, huge corporations like Amazon do not arise in a social vacuum. We know that markets are always manufactured, and contrary to economist Friedrich

Introduction 3

Hayek's stance, they are created by clear economic and political choices in a given society.[7] This book argues that Amazon did not become the powerful global giant it is because of its "disruptive" and "innovative" character but because of decades of laissez-faire regulations measures, decreased antitrust oversight, and unequal wealth distribution frameworks (taxation *in primis*). By looking at Amazon as a global giant that is crucially embedded in the capitalist systems where it operates, we examine the corporation as a site where business and cultural strategies, capital structures, ownership and control, public relation efforts, and the state all interact.

While PEC sets the framework of this book, four additional theoretical perspectives are extremely relevant for an analysis of Amazon. These concepts are concentration, data extraction, rent in the digital economy, and network effect. Together, they underlie the central hypothesis of the book: that Amazon has become a *Global Communication Giant and a Digital Lord.*

Political economists have long explored the issue of *concentration* in the communication industry, focusing on forms of concentration that distort market systems.[8] Organisations that are too large or that operate as monopolies reduce competition and restrict innovation, thus interrupting the free flow of market forces, while at the same time wielding their intrinsic power to direct politics and policy making. Concentration thus becomes a crucial concept to understand the basic power relations and capitalist structure in which new Internet platforms have been developed and thrive.[9]

Other business and political economy studies have looked at significant *network effects* in the adoption of technology products and services. Major studies such as Katz and Shapiro[10] and Liebowitz and Margolis[11] demonstrate that the more users a digital service attracts, the more the value is increased. In other words, the utility of the goods increases with the number of users. The bigger the network, the bigger the return on some services. Scholars also distinguish between two types of network effects:[12] direct and indirect. Direct is strictly linked to the number of adopters on the intrinsic value of the product. Indirect network effects are due to the secondary effect caused by the cumulative number of users, for example, obtained or triggered by players on the other side of the market. One example is an increase in the range of matching components related to the core product or service, which in turn increases the value of the core product or service. These concepts become of great relevance in understanding how Internet platforms work in the context of capitalism and certainly are crucial in comprehending the strategies of growth of Amazon. The more Internet platforms are used and the more users they have, the more interesting they become for returning users and the more challenging for smaller providers to compete. As I argue in Chapter 2, the influence and size of the pool of users and

4 *Benedetta Brevini*

reputation also trigger indirect network effects activated by other players operating in the same markets but with different objectives (consider, for example, other producers or other sellers or advertisers).

From a different scholarly perspective, economist Mariana Mazzucato[13] argues that if we are really to understand the sources of power inequalities in our economy, we need to focus on *rents*.[14] As Adam Smith explained, rent is a monopoly price. Smith used the example of land/real estate to explain the ways in which owners can extract money from consumers, which is neither payment for labour nor for necessary capital.[15] In other words, rent can be conceived as merely "value extraction" without production involved. Rents are tightly connected to the network effect: it is predictable that in the presence of a legal vacuum, new Internet platforms, enjoying strong network effects, will become conglomerates that can generate massive rents. As Tim O'Reilly warns: "control that the platforms have over placement and visibility puts them in a unique position to collect what economists call *rents*: that is, value extracted through the ownership of a limited resource".[16] The concept of rent helps explain Amazon's global success: the company charges *rent* to all third-party sellers, but Amazon's own products use the company platforms without fees.

Data extraction and circulation are also central elements of the current structure of capitalism. As Mosco succinctly says,

> The Next Internet brings together three interconnected systems: cloud computing, big data analytics, and the Internet of Things. It promises centralized data storage and services in vast digital factories that process massive streams of information gathered by networked sensors stored in every possible consumer, industrial, and office device, as well as in living bodies.[17]

So, it would be impossible to understand Amazon without pondering on its insatiable hunger to accumulate data, which has become the new established norm of doing business.[18] The more data Amazon collects, the more it is able to produce an accurate profile of its customers, thus attracting more users and sellers. This in turn assists machine learning and helps lock users into the company's Digital Estate.

Political economic relations that put data at centre stage use a variety of labels – including Fuchs' *Big Data Capitalism*[19] and Zuboff's[20] *Surveillance Capitalism*, drawing upon previous work on the role of data and surveillance by Gandy[21] and Foster and McChesney[22] to the more recent *Platform Capitalism* by Srnicek.[23] The common themes of these works are that data has a crucial value, data collection is highly unequal and tends to replicate

Introduction 5

the same power asymmetries in societies, and also that extraction has a major bearing on the way in which corporation and governments behave.

Drawing on these frameworks, the book argues that Amazon has relentlessly moved to become a *Global Communication Giant and a Digital Lord* that has and continues to exploit a technological infrastructure built on public resources: the Internet. Contrary to what major Silicon Valley giants argue when they claim ownership of innovation, we should never forget that most of the major inventions on which tech giants rely came from public resources and long-term government investments. The Internet is certainly one of the most radical of such ideas and was possible only because of decades of public resources and planning. However, the success of Amazon is based on the Internet's specific and intrinsic network effects, the capitalisation of its rents, the extraction of data, and the monopolisation of scarce resources that stifles competition.

This study draws heavily upon document research and adopts both primary and secondary sources from:

- Corporate annual reports, including Amazon's quarterly reports and other forms of trade releases from related companies' policy documents from American and European institutions – the U.S. Securities and Exchange Commission, the U.S. federal government, state governments, and the European Commission
- News reports and analysis, business and trade sources
- Reports from professional investment analysts, audit reports, and independent assessments

Chapter 2, "Economic Profile", highlights the historical context and economic characteristics of Amazon, its business strategies, and relentless expansion to become with time one of the leading Global Communication Giants. Chapter 3, "Political Profile", delves into the company's complex ownership and organisation, and primary institutional stakeholders' ties to powerful elites. It also describes the most relevant political controversies in which Amazon was at centre stage, starting with the battles to improve the labour conditions in its warehouses. Chapter 4 focuses on the most popular and successful products by Amazon, the company's symbolic universe, and the ideology that drives it. Chapter 5, the concluding chapter, elaborates on Amazon's political, economic, and cultural profiles that together explain the birth and growth of one of the most successful tech giants of the West. It also adopts a metaphor that is useful to understand the extent, reach, and features of the global success of Amazon. Amazon has become a Digital Lord.

Notes

1. www.independent.co.uk/news/world/americas/coronavirus-amazon-jeff-bezos-relief-fund-covid-19-billionaire-net-worth-a9422236.html.
2. www.bloomberg.com/billionaires/.
3. www.cnbc.com/2020/03/26/amazon-warehouse-employees-grapple-with-coronavirus-risks.html.
4. Reich, R. (2007). *Supercapitalism. The transformation of business, democracy and everyday life*. New York: Vintage.
5. https://naomiklein.org/the-shock-doctrine/.
6. Mosco, V. (2008). Current trends in the political economy of communication. *Global Media Journal*, 1, 45.
7. Hayek, F. A. (2014). *The road to serfdom: Text and documents: The definitive edition*. New York: Routledge.
8. Murdock, G., & Golding, P. (1973). For a political economy of mass communications. *Socialist Register*, 10, 205–234.
9. See, for example, work by McChesney, R. (2013). *Digital disconnect: How capitalism is turning the internet against democracy*. New York: New Press; Mosco, V. (2014). *To the cloud: Big data in a turbulent world*. Boulder, CO: Paradigm.
10. Katz, M. L., & Shapiro, C. (1986). Technology adoption in the presence of network externalities. *Journal of Political Economy*, 94(4), 822–841.
11. Liebowitz, S. J., & Margolis, S. E. (1994). Network externality: An uncommon tragedy. *Journal of Economic Perspectives*, 8(2), 133–150.
12. Ibid.; Katz & Shapiro (1986) op. cit.
13. Mazzucato, M. (2018). *The value of everything: Making and taking in the global economy*. London: Hachette.
14. Lackman, C. L. (1976). The classical base of modem rent theory. *American Journal of Economics and Sociology*, 35(3), 287–300.
15. Ibid.
16. https://qz.com/1666863/why-big-tech-keeps-outsmarting-antitrust-regulators/.
17. Mosco, V. (2017). The next internet. In *Carbon capitalism and communication* (pp. 95–107). Cham: Palgrave Macmillan.
18. Mayer-Schoenberger, V., & Cukier, K. (2013). *Big data. A revolution that will transform how we live, work, and think*. London: John Murray Publishers.
19. Fuchs, C. (2019). Karl Marx in the age of big data capitalism. In D. Chandler & C. Fuchs (Eds.), *Digital objects, digital subjects: Interdisciplinary perspectives on capitalism, labour and politics in the age of big data* (pp. 53–71). London: University of Westminster Press.
20. Zuboff, S. (2019). *The age of surveillance capitalism: The fight for a human future at the new frontier of power*. London: Profile Books.
21. Gandy, O. H. (1993). *The panoptic sort: A political economy of personal information*. Boulder, CO: Westview Press.
22. Foster, J. B., & McChesney, R. W. (2014). Surveillance capitalism: Monopoly-finance capital, the military-industrial complex, and the digital age. *Monthly Review*, 66(3), 1.
23. Srnicek, N. (2017). *Platform capitalism*. New York: John Wiley & Sons.

2 Economic Profile

Benedetta Brevini

This chapter aims to dissect, analyse, and understand the complex web of economic influence of Amazon. It will examine its economic profile and profit-maximisation strategies to show why its constant focus on making low profits on many items, rather than high profits on a few, became the core strategy to build its platform. The chapter will delve into its core "product as service" strategy, exploring the courses of integration and diversification as the company develops into the global communication giant we know today.

History of Economic Success

With its $280.5 billion in revenue at the beginning of 2020, Amazon has joined the $1 trillion market capitalisation club with the other tech giants Microsoft, Alphabet, and Apple, with an average annual revenue growth rate of 26.9% over the last five years.

To many loyal customers, Amazon.com is one of the most established online retailers, although as this chapter will establish, it is much more than that: its biggest success is currently its service department, especially its cloud services branch (AWS) which achieved impressive growth in the last decade, doubling its earnings in the last two years.

Amazon is ranked fourth on *Forbes*'s list of World's Most Valuable Brands 2019, before Facebook (5), Coca-Cola (6), and Disney (8). Its global economic impact is striking. While the company has its major headquarters in Seattle, Washington, it employs over 798,000 people full-time and part-time worldwide (as of December 31, 2019).[1] This figure is expected to grow exponentially both in the United States and internationally. Employment levels fluctuate due to seasonal factors affecting the business, yet the tech giant employs more people than its three largest competitors combined: Alphabet (Google) boasts 94,000 employees, while Facebook employs 33,000 staff, and Microsoft's workforce amounts to 140,000. Its extraordinary growth

8 Benedetta Brevini

has been a constant feature of Amazon since its birth. By the end of 1996, one year after its launch, Amazon had rented a 93,000-square-foot warehouse, quickly leaving its small garage, and had sold more than $16 million worth of books to nearly 200,000 customers in over 100 countries.[2]

The company was publicly listed in May 1997 at $18 per share with a market capitalisation of $429 million; one year after it went public, stocks were selling at $105 per share, valuing the company at $5 billion.[3]

Sales have seen steady growth over recent years, and Amazon has gone from selling $5 million worth of books in 1995 to nearly $280.52 billion in product and service net revenues in 2020. This growth is illustrated in Figure 2.1.

Despite its international expansion (the first international Amazon domains, Amazon.co.uk and Amazon.de, went online in 1998), Amazon still offers more services in North America than worldwide. As a result, the majority of the company's net revenue in 2019 was actually earned in the United States and Canada. In 2019, approximately US $170.77 billion was earned in North America compared to US $74.7 billion internationally.

From its 10-K forms, Amazon is adamant that it organises its operations into three segments: North America, International, and Amazon Web Services (AWS).

This obviously means that data for each specific branch and subsidiary of the company are not really accessible. However, a closer look at the company

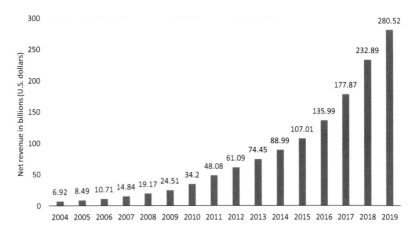

Figure 2.1 Revenue Net Income Total Assets: 2004–2019

Sources: Amazon.com, Inc., Form 10-K, 2004–2019

Economic Profile 9

statements is revealing of the incredible disparity in earnings of the different entities. Some divisions have small and steady earnings, while others are generating massive profits and running major investments in technology.

Beyond Retail: Amazon the Global Communication Giant

The differentiation between products and services is the distinction Amazon makes when filing 10-K forms with the Securities and Exchange Commission. From the 10-K form we learn that for the company,

> Product sales represent revenue from the sale of products and related shipping fees and digital media content where we record revenue gross. Service sales primarily represent third-party seller fees, which includes commissions and any related fulfillment and shipping fees, AWS sales, Amazon Prime membership fees, advertising services, and certain digital content subscriptions.[4]

From the 2020 reports (Table 2.1) we learn that Amazon's total sales reached $280.52 billion in 2019, a 20.5% increase from $232.89 in 2018. Of that revenue, $160.41 billion was categorised as "product sales", driving an increase of 13.0% year-over-year from $141.92 billion.

But it's really in the "service sales" that the incredible success of Amazon can be assessed.

The $120.11 billion in sales came from commissions from outside sellers that sell on Amazon marketplaces, advertising services, and the highly profitable Amazon Web Services (AWS), offering cloud computing services. Service sales more than doubled in less than two years from $59.293 billion in 2017 to $90.97 billion in 2019.

A closer look at Amazon Web Service shows that its revenues hit $35.03 billion, up 36.5% from $25.66 billion a year earlier. Although net sales from AWS are far below North America's figures (Table 2.3), AWS

Table 2.1 Consolidated Statements

	Year Ended December 31					
	2017		2018		2019	
Net product sales	$	118,573	$	141,915	$	160,408
Net service sales		59,293		90,972		120,114
Total net sales		177,866		232,887		280,522

Source: Amazon

10 *Benedetta Brevini*

Table 2.2 Net Sales of the Three Divisions and AWS Sales

	Year Ended December 31			
	2018		*2019*	
Net sales:				
North America	$	141,366	$	170,773
International		65,866		74,723
AWS		25,655		35,026
Consolidated		**232,887**		**280,522**
Year-over-year percentage growth:				
North America		33%		21%
International		21		13
AWS		47		37
Consolidated		31		20

Source: Amazon

Table 2.3 Operating Income (Profits) Three Business Divisions: Amazon

	Year Ended December 31			
	2018		*2019*	
Operating income				
North America	$	7,267	$	7,033
International		(2,142)		(1,693)
AWS		7,296		9,201
Consolidated		**12,421**		**14,541**

has overtaken North America in operating income: as per Table 2.4, AWS earned $9.20 billion in operating income, or two-thirds of the $14.54 billion in operating income for 2019.

The two divisions came very close to generating the same amount of operating income in 2018: 50.1% for AWS as compared with 49.9% for North America. AWS's clientele includes big business, government agencies, and academic institutions, helping them store massive amounts of information and deliver content – what Amazon calls a "broad set of global compute, storage database, and other service offerings".[5]

Amazon Marketplace, Data, and the Success of Third-Party Sellers: The Birth of a Giant

Over the last 15 years, the success of Amazon as a global communication service company has been more and more integrated with its prosperous

Economic Profile 11

Table 2.4 Net Sales by Group of Similar Products and Services

	Year Ended December 31					
	2017		2018		2019	
Net sales:						
Online stores (1)	$	108,354	$	122,987	$	141,247
Physical stores (2)		5,798		17,224		17,192
Third-party seller services (3)		31,881		42,745		53,762
Subscription services (4)		9,721		14,168		19,210
AWS		17,459		25,655		35,026
Other (5)		4,653		10,108		14,085
Consolidated		**177,866**		**232,887**		**280,522**

Source: Amazon

"third-party seller service" division. Amazon accounts for third-party sales on a net basis, not a gross basis. This means that it reports only the actual returns made on those sales, which almost doubled in two years from 2017 to 2019 (see Table 2.4).

So why is Amazon encouraging the development of a third-party market even more than its own online retail business? The answer is twofold: money and data – which turns into money.

In fact, Amazon takes a percentage of each third-party sale, plus additional fees to store and ship the inventory of the merchants, which use the Fulfilled by Amazon service and often the additional advertising services (listed under "Other" in Table 2.4, which also registered impressive growth). Moreover, the online sales division by Amazon also benefits from third-party sales. In fact, as Calabrese and Rollins note:

> While the marketplace does offer increased traffic to third parties, these sellers have difficulty securing repeat customers because so many view Amazon sellers as homogeneous. That is, there is no reason to be loyal to a particular seller on Amazon because the service is relatively similar, as are prices, across sellers. Further, Amazon often offers the same products as third parties for a lower price or with preferred webpage placement. This has led some sellers to see a decline in sales as they are put into competition directly with Amazon.[6]

But there is another reason for Amazon to invest so heavily in the marketplace: data. While Amazon gets all data from its marketplace sellers, these sellers don't get access to their customer data. So, on the one hand, Amazon increases its network and customer base because customers still understand their purchase to have been made with Amazon.com, a situation that

12 *Benedetta Brevini*

rewards Amazon with returning customers. On the other hand, all customer data and consumer profiles are in the hands of Amazon. Amazon then uses this data to deliver other services: not just advertising products (discussed at the end of this chapter) but also offering new devices and technology, like Alexa.

A letter from Jeff Bezos to his shareholders sent at the beginning of 2019 invites shareowners to consider the incredible growth of third-party sales. It was a move that has been described by many as an attempt to respond to antitrust critiques moved by Senator Elizabeth Warren. Bezos invites the shareholders to take a look at these numbers:

1999	3%
2000	3%
2001	6%
2002	17%
2003	22%
2004	25%
2005	28%
2006	28%
2007	29%
2008	30%
2009	31%
2010	34%
2011	38%
2012	42%
2013	46%
2014	49%
2015	51%
2016	54%
2017	56%
2018	58%

The percentages represent the share of physical gross merchandise sales sold on Amazon by independent third-party sellers – mostly small- and medium-sized businesses – as opposed to Amazon retail's own first party sales. Third-party sales have grown from 3% of the total to 58%. To put it bluntly: Third-party sellers are kicking our first party butt. Badly.[7]

This is not really the full story. By developing a stronger marketplace of sellers that become dependent and stuck in Amazon's ecosystem, Amazon develops its platform.

Economic Profile 13

Understanding Amazon Kingdom: The Communication Giant

As noted, Amazon has organised its global activities around three branches: North America, International, and Amazon Web Services. Senior management teams include three CEOs and three senior vice presidents responsible for various crucial aspects of the business, reporting directly to Amazon CEO Jeff Bezos. Continuity in top management, as we will see in Chapter 3, is a key feature of Amazon, with little turnover among its most important players. Amazon's organisational structure integrates many small teams that deal with various aspects of the business. Founder and CEO Jeff Bezos is credited with the introduction of the "two pizza rule": meetings should be held in teams small enough that all could be fed with only two pizzas.

Back in 1999, when the world was looking at Amazon as an online retail platform, Bezos was explaining Amazon's focus:

> Sometimes people ask us, are you a book company or a music company, or now are you a toy company or . . . ? And we're none of those things. We're trying to be a customer company. And you can sort of uniquely do that well on the internet because of the possibilities for personalization, and you know, putting each individual customer at the center of your universe. And if you can do that, you'll have something completely new.[8]

Today, few universes of business are untouched by Amazon. One might be using an app that relies on Amazon services, shopping on an Amazon platform or many of Amazon's web services without knowing.

Here I provide an overview of some of the most relevant sectors of the Amazon realm, stretching from technology services (including facial recognition, cloud computing, home security, micro labour tasks, and home products powered by AI) to publishing, logistics, advertising business, media, television, and films. On their own, all of these companies have targeted markets. But together, under the same platform, they reinforce each other's powers. For example, Prime members (discussed later) have access to free shipping options but get also access to Prime Music, Video, Food Services, and Media. Amazon's strategy does not aim to make extreme margins on individual sales but to offer services instead, to lock the customer in the Amazon realm forever.

Like other digital giants, Amazon companies have begun developing products that are designed to be a service platform – so instead of a single purchase or one-time fee, they encourage customers to take a monthly subscription. This is not divergent from similar "tech-centric" Internet

14 *Benedetta Brevini*

businesses and corporations, including Apple and Microsoft, where the product delivery is centred on subscription-based services that are inherently designed to entice and capture a consumer, to lock them into a specific ecosystem.

As we will see, the use of artificial intelligence (AI) through the Alexa product line is a core example of this: whereby goods can be bought from Amazon's marketplace(s) directly through the voice assistant, and services such as Prime Video, Amazon Music Audible, and Twitch are integrated into these physical devices, further encouraging consumers to remain subscribed. This means sharing their data – what music they listen to, which video games interest them – which is stored in the same consumer directory that records what they buy on Amazon.

Technology, AI, Cloud, and Digital Products

Amazon Robotics, originally Kiva Systems, designs and manufactures robots to help with product fulfilment systems. Prior to its acquisition by Amazon, Kiva held contracts with other consumer goods chains, including Walgreens; following the Amazon takeover those contracts were not renewed, nor was the technology available outside Amazon.[9]

Amazon utilises the products/technologies designed in-house to "make every product mobile" on the warehouse floor, which Amazon says reduces the time that employees spend walking. Amazon further states that the use of robotics also allows greater efficiency in warehouse storage and can move up to 340kgs of goods at once. Amazon claims that it does not prefer robots over humans for many jobs and advertises that it has created over 300,000 positions in distribution since the introduction of robots in 2012.[10]

Hardware

In 2004, Amazon opened Lab126, a computer hardware research and development unit. The California-based laboratory has developed some of Amazon's most successful products, including Kindle and its many new versions.

Security and AI

Amazon's AI technology, Alexa, was the first virtual assistant developed by Amazon. It also acquired two security companies: Blink Home, a home security company that makes automated security cameras and video doorbells, and Ring, known for its smart doorbell, currently being marketed to local police units.

Economic Profile 15

Audible

Audible is an online digital distribution service for spoken audio content, primarily audiobooks. Via an in-house publishing service, Audible has also become the largest producer of audiobooks. Like many companies within the Amazon ecosystem, Audible offers a subscription service, although individual audiobooks are available for purchase. Audible is well integrated into the Amazon product ecosystem, with features like Whispersync, which ties into the Kindle e-book version 8,[11] as well as core integration Echo smart devices and Alexa AI assistant integration.[12] Amazon also acquired Brilliance Audio in 2007, then the largest independent publisher of audiobooks in the U.S.[13]

Amazon Web Services

As discussed in the previous section, Amazon Web Services is a subsidiary of Amazon Inc that develops and maintains numerous services of ICT infrastructure (cloud computing) to governments, businesses, and individuals worldwide. AWS summarises its services as "cloud-based products including compute, storage, databases, analytics, networking, mobile, developer tools, management tools, IoT, security, and enterprise applications: on-demand, available in seconds, with pay-as-you-go pricing".[14] Physical infrastructure like server farms are located in numerous countries worldwide, allowing for businesses to locate their rented infrastructure geographically nearby.[15] In 2017, AWS was estimated to have a 34% market share in the cloud computing space, nearly triple its next nearest competitor, Microsoft's Azure platform.[16] "The AWS Cloud spans 60 Availability Zones within 20 geographic Regions around the world, with announced plans for 12 more Availability Zones and four more Regions in Bahrain, Cape Town, Hong Kong SAR, and Milan".[17]

Publishing

Amazon's origin as an online book retailer in 1994 has stayed with the media giant despite its new ventures. It still has several bookselling and publishing subsidiaries, most of which now fall under the umbrella of Amazon Publishing. This division publishes and owns imprints for specific genres, languages, and locales.

AbeBooks and Book Depository are both Amazon subsidiaries and were the first competitors for books and similar products; ComiXolog, an online distribution service for comic books, similar to Amazon's Kindle service or Apple's iBooks, was acquired by Amazon in April 2014.[18] ComiXology is

16 *Benedetta Brevini*

one of the Amazon subsidiaries that offers a subscription service, which is tied into Amazon's greater offerings, reinforcing the ecosystem of the platform, with the platform-agnostic product having special features on Amazon's Kindle devices.[19]

DP Review was founded in 1998 as a website to review digital cameras and other related equipment acquired by Amazon in 2007.[20]

Goodreads is a book review aggregator with social media style functionality allowing for the creation of personal, public-facing catalogues and libraries. Purchased by Amazon in 2013 for $150 million, Goodreads currently boasts 80 million members and 2.3 million books in its database, according to its website.[21] Goodreads has direct tie-ins to other parts of the Amazon ecosystem, including Audible, Kindle/e-book devices and Book Depository. Data collection from Goodreads further helps the corporation target specific books to customers, as well as provide essential statistics and reviews to the publishing industry and for Amazon's data analytics segment. Amazon's control and ownership of Goodreads and its data further cements Amazon's dominance over its rivals in bookselling, such as Barnes and Noble in the U.S.[22]

Media, Games, and Music

IMDb, or Internet Movie Database, is a database of film and television and an authoritative website source for Western movies and television content. Acquired by Amazon in 1998,[23] IMDb has an Alexa rank of 49.[24] Through its internal ratings system[25] and comprehensive data on cast and crew, IMDb has become a staple not only for consumers of film and television but for the industry. After acquiring IMDb, Amazon led its expansion into music. At its launch, the site offered users more than 125,000 CD and DVD titles. The following year, Amazon acquired Alexa Internet, a web traffic analysis company – not to be confused with the other, more popular Alexa that came later. It wasn't until 2007 that Amazon launched its streaming service, Amazon MP3, which later became Amazon Music. In 2006, the company launched Amazon Unbox, a service for purchasing and downloading videos, which was later changed to Amazon Video on Demand, then Amazon Instant Video, and finally Prime Video. Prime Video showcases content by Amazon Studios, which began in 2010 as a script development entity but now produces and distributes television series and films. In 2017, Amazon Studios purchased the TV rights to a *Lord of the Rings* spinoff for an estimated $250 million. Through IMDb, Amazon also purchased Withoutabox, which streamlined the submission and selection process for film festivals (and which Amazon is in the process of closing), as well as Box Office Mojo, which algorithmically tracks box office revenue, in 2008.

Twitch

Amazon also owns Twitch, the premier online video "live-streaming" service,[26] with a major focus on the video game community, e-sports, and other video game-related content. Twitch has also seen the rise of "adult/mature" entertainment,[27] which has raised controversy within the community due to the lack of regulation such as age-verification, as well as live-streaming of real-world activities like travelling, eating, or cooking.[28] Twitch was purchased by Amazon in August 2014 for $970 million[29] after a substantive bidding war against Google[30] and allegedly Microsoft.[31] Further, community perceptions of bias within Twitch management as to which content/ personalities to enforce regulations on has damaged the reputation of the brand – although there is minimal evidence of this bias occurring.[32] Twitch claims to have "millions" of regular users,[33] with an estimated 1 million concurrent users, and 15 million per day, making it one of the largest digital media sites. Twitch is further evidence of Amazon's "services as a platform" mentality, with there being significant incentives, both on-platform and with partner websites and services, for Twitch users to have an Amazon Prime account and vice-versa.[34] Twitch also possesses a digital distribution service for video games and further hosts and distributes the largest repository of third-party modifications and add-ons for video games via its desktop client.[35]

Retail

As we have seen, Amazon has more than 6 million independent merchants that pay to sell goods through Amazon's e-commerce marketplace, with many others also shelling out additional fees for logistical services like shipping and warehousing. Beyond services and e-commerce, Amazon also manufactures and promotes its own products with a set of house brands. These include Mountain Falls, which primarily creates personal care products, furniture brand Rivet, and women's clothing line Daily Ritual. Amazon Basics also exists to offer Amazon-brand alternatives to popular marketplace products.

Additionally, Amazon acquired supermarket chain Whole Foods in mid-2017 for $13.4 billion in an attempt to "turn Amazon into a more frequent shopping habit by becoming a bigger player in food and beverages".[36] Coupled with Amazon's "Go" supermarket chain, the purchase of Whole Foods was further described by *The New York Times* as an attempt to counter Walmart, Amazon's main rival for market share, from making further inroads into the food and grocery market in the U.S.[37] Whole Foods was quickly integrated with Amazon's Prime services, which promote brand

18   *Benedetta Brevini*

goods for sale on Amazon's website as well as various delivery benefits in certain U.S. cities.[38] This acquisition and integration of Whole Foods not only provides Amazon with a significant brick and mortar footprint in the United States, United Kingdom, and Canada, but also places it in the top five grocery retailers in the U.S. This crucial acquisition allowed the corporation to expand its data extraction even further, which became the fundamental capital to exploit when developing its most recent venture: advertising.

Amazon's expansion into advertising sales is among its biggest recent initiatives, consistent with its continually setting itself up in competition with Facebook and Alphabet's Google. Amazon's advertising promotes products by third-party partner vendors both within and outside of the Amazon platform. As discussed in Chapter 4, Amazon's powerful brand recognition and dominance means it can offer retailers a substantial return on investment (ROI). Amazon's advertising growth is difficult to quantify as its annual reports combine its advertising sales figures with other undisclosed service sales under "Other", as seen in Table 2.4. However, it is clear this business has been among Amazon's fastest growing. Amazon Advertising is now the third-largest digital advertising platform, behind Google and Facebook, with an estimated 4.2% market share.

Finally, Amazon Prime represents the most successful example of the strategy of building loyal, repeat customers who, instead of buying a product, buy a long-term service from Amazon, thus getting locked into the platform.

Prime is a subscription service that facilitates discounted and expedited shipping on products bought via Amazon or via third parties with stock present in its distribution networks. Prime is an exceedingly popular service, with approximately 100 million customers worldwide by the middle of 2018, with 10% growth from 2017 numbers.[39] Prime offers access to most of the Amazon network and is central to Amazon's "services as a product" strategy. In the United States, the Prime service offers same-day delivery, including two-hour delivery in numerous U.S. metro centres. By offering these features, it encourages customers to utilise Amazon as a first stop of preference for shopping and stay as loyal serfs, locked in forever.

In an attempt to create a "shopping holiday", Amazon created what it dubbed "Prime Day", designed to mimic the retail sector's "Black Friday" – a shopping holiday that originated in the United States, the day after Thanksgiving. Amazon's pilot "Prime Day" broke sales records, even exceeding sales on Black Friday 2014, which had been the biggest Black Friday to date.[40] Amazon ensures that to reap what would be perceived as the full value of "Prime Day", a Prime membership is required – indeed, the deals are only available to Prime members.[41]

Developing Economies: Expanding Its Influence

While Amazon is leading Western markets, competitors are now emerging from international markets, including China, which pose a serious challenge to Amazon's dominance. This is due in large part to their ability to provide lower-cost items such as consumer electronics and clothing. Budget e-commerce sites such as AliExpress, Taobao, and Banggood already occupy the budget offering space; in fact, many of the products available on Amazon are simply branded and/or higher-priced variants of products on competing Chinese platforms.

AliExpress is of particular note, as it is expressly designed to be a foreign-facing platform for Chinese sellers and manufacturers (Chinese users cannot access the platform), though it is closer to eBay than Amazon, acting as an intermediary rather than a fulfilment service and producer.

Chinese alternatives possess numerous economic advantages over Amazon. While it would be a stretch to say the competition is "fair" in terms of trade, Chinese warehouses have access to cheaper labour and space, and those employed are under Chinese labour laws. Shipping is further heavily subsidised worldwide by China Post, and particularly in Asia, shipping times are lower than for products coming from North America or Europe.

AliExpress's recently announced expansion to support EU-based sellers further risks Amazon's dominance in the global marketplace. Alibaba is further expected to overtake Amazon as the largest e-commerce platform in 2019.[42] Chinese alternatives are at times more competitive marketplaces to the consumer, not just in Asia but in Amazon's primary Western market.

Amazon itself has withdrawn from supporting third-party sellers in the Chinese market, following substantial difficulties in launching and stiff competition in the domestic market. While Amazon bought joyo.com, giving it market space within China, according to a market intelligence company, Amazon never saw its market share go above 6% of the e-commerce space within the country.[43]

While Amazon's purchase of souk.com showed an ability to absorb the competition in some global regions, Asia has proven more difficult territory. With the rising economic power of other nations such as India (with domestic e-commerce sites like Flipkart and PayTM) and Indonesia (Tokopedia), largely due to the growing middle class, domestic marketplaces in those countries may well be able to compete on a global level within the coming decade. In Southeast Asian markets, apart from domestic offerings, Alibaba/AliExpress represent the current market shareholder in the region and for the reasons noted previously offer a much more competitive price for the middle class. This is particularly significant because these markets represent the greatest opportunity for growth for Amazon.

20 *Benedetta Brevini*

Notes

1. Amazon 10-K form. https://ir.aboutamazon.com/sec-filings/sec-filings-details/ default.aspx?FilingId=13875159.
2. Calabrese, A., & Rollins, T. (2016). Amazon. com. In *Global media giants* (pp. 427–441). New York: Routledge.
3. Ibid.
4. Amazon 10-K form, p. 19 op. cit.
5. Ibid., p. 3.
6. Calabrese & Rollins (2016) op. cit.
7. Bezos, J. P. (2018). *2018 Letter to Shareholders*. https://www.sec.gov/Archives/ edgar/data/1018724/000119312519103013/d727605dex991.htm.
8. Jeff Bezos interviewed by David and Tom Gardner on the Motley Fool Radio show in 1999. https://www.youtube.com/watch?v=HqisHKpFgnM.
9. Supply Chain News. (2014, March 31). Amazon will not make Kiva Systems available to general market for at least two years. www.scdigest.com/ontarget/ 14-03-31-1.php?cid=7944.
10. 5 facts to know about Amazon Robotics. https://blog.aboutamazon.eu/innova tion/5-facts-to-know-about-amazon-robotics.
11. Audible. What is Whispersync voice. https://audible.custhelp.com/app/answers/ detail/a_id/7371/kw/whispersync.
12. ZDNet. Amazon Echo now reads Audible books to you. www.zdnet.com/ article/amazon-echo-now-reads-audible-books-to-you/.
13. Taume News. (2007, May 27). Amazon acquires brilliance audio. https://web. archive.org/web/20070704192411/http://news.taume.com/World-Business/ Business-Finance/Amazon_com-Acquires-Brilliance-Audio-1358.
14. AWS. (2018, December). Overview of Amazon Web Services, p. 1. https:// d1.awsstatic.com/whitepapers/aws-overview.pdf.
15. AWS. About AWS. https://aws.amazon.com/about-aws/.
16. AWS Insider. (2017, August 1). https://awsinsider.net/articles/2017/08/01/aws-market-share-3x-azure.aspx.
17. AWS Security. Global infrastructure. https://aws.amazon.com/security/.
18. Comixology. (2014, April 10). Message to our customers. www.comixology. com/message.
19. Amazon. ComiXology unlimited. www.amazon.com/ComiXology-Unlimited-Kindle-Store/b?node=14567849011.
20. DPReview. (2007, May 14). Amazon acquires DPReview. www.dpreview. com/articles/1690663587/amazonacquiresdpreview.
21. Goodreads. About Us. www.goodreads.com/about/us.
22. The Atlantic. (2013, April 1). The simple reason why Goodreads is so valuable to Amazon. www.theatlantic.com/business/archive/2013/04/the-simple-reason-why-goodreads-is-so-valuable-to-amazon/274548/.
23. IMDb. What is IMDb? https://help.imdb.com/article/imdb/general-information/ what-is-imdb/G836CY29Z4SGNMK5?ref_=helpart_nav_1#.
24. Alexa Internet. IMDb rank. www.alexa.com/siteinfo/imdb.com.
25. IMDb. FAQ for IMDb ratings. https://help.imdb.com/article/imdb/track-movies-tv/faq-for-imdb-ratings/G67Y87TFYYP6TWAV#.
26. Alexa Internet. (2019, January 11). Twitch.tv Site info. www.alexa.com/site info/twitch.tv.

Economic Profile 21

27. The Guardian. (2017, January 3). The women who make a living gaming on Twitch. www.theguardian.com/technology/2017/jan/03/women-make-living-gaming-twitch.
28. The Verge. (2016, December 15). Twitch's new IRL category is for streaming everyday life stuff. www.theverge.com/2016/12/15/13967550/twitch-new-irl-category-streaming-real-life.
29. Twitch.tv Blog. A letter from the CEO. https://blog.twitch.tv/a-letter-from-the-ceo-august-25-2014-b34c1cfbb099.
30. The Guardian. Twitch: What is it, and why has Google bought it for $1bn? www.theguardian.com/technology/2014/jul/25/twitch-google-gaming-video-site.
31. Business Insider. (2014, August 26). Amazon buys Twitch. www.businessinsider.com.au/amazon-buys-twitch-2014-8.
32. Mashable.com. (2019, February 14). Deadmau5 tries to defend using homophobic slur after Twitch ban. https://mashable.com/article/deadmau5-homophobic-slur-twitch-ban/#Bi0WRZNfZGq7.
33. Twitch.tv About Us. www.twitch.tv/p/about/.
34. Twitch.tv About Twitch Prime. https://help.twitch.tv/customer/portal/articles/2572060-twitch-prime-guide.
35. Curseforge Authors. https://authors.curseforge.com.
36. New York Times. (2017, June 16). Amazon to buy Whole Foods. www.nytimes.com/2017/06/16/business/dealbook/amazon-whole-foods.html.
37. Ibid.
38. Amazon. (2017). Annual report. https://ir.aboutamazon.com/static-files/917130c5-e6bf-4790-a7bc-cc43ac7fb30a.
39. Business Insider. (2018, April 19). Amazon Prime member numbers revealed. www.businessinsider.com.au/amazon-prime-member-numbers-revealed-2018-4?op=1&r=US&IR=T.
40. Techcrunch.com Amazon says Prime Day was bigger than Black Friday and will be held again 16 July 2015. https://techcrunch.com/2015/07/16/amazon-says-prime-day-was-bigger-than-black-friday-and-will-be-held-again/.
41. Amazon. Prime Day. www.amazon.com/Prime-Day/b?node=13887280011.
42. Engadget. (2019, May 5). Alibaba opens e-commerce platform to sellers outside of China. www.engadget.com/2019/05/09/alibaba-opens-ali-express-to-retailers-outside-China/.
43. CBS News. (2019, April 19). In rare defeat, Amazon retreats from its China business. www.cbsnews.com/news/amazon-will-no-longer-sell-chinese-goods-in-china/.

3 Political Profile

Benedetta Brevini and Lukasz Swiatek

This chapter explores Amazon's ownership, corporate governance (focusing on its board of directors and interlocks), multidimensional political agenda, growing political connections, and the major labour controversies that have surrounded it. These intricate relationships, loyalties, and connections have helped the organisation expand its influence.

Ownership

Jeff Bezos has served as the CEO and chairman of Amazon since its inception. He has also remained Amazon's biggest stakeholder, owning over 55 million shares: approximately 11% of the organisation's total shares as of March 2020.[1] Although Bezos holds more Amazon stock than any other individual – as shown in Table 3.1 – he boasts never to have received any stock-based compensation from Amazon and receives a small executive salary of $81,840. However, according to the U.S. Securities and Exchange Commission, Bezos has sold more than 18.5 million shares of his company over the last ten years,[2] making huge profits in light of the fact that between January 2015 and December 2019, Amazon's stocks rose approximately 495%, while the S&P 500 rose approximately 57%. Bezos is also the founder of the aerospace company Blue Origin, which is working to lower the cost and increase the safety of spaceflight; additionally, he is the owner of *The Washington Post* newspaper.[3] With a personal wealth of $145 billion, he is believed to be the wealthiest person on the planet, according to *Forbes*.[4]

Bezos's net worth took a hit in 2019, however, after he announced his divorce from his wife, MacKenzie Bezos. At the time, the couple held 78.8 million shares in Amazon. As part of the settlement, Bezos kept the entirety of the couple's stake in *The Washington Post* and Blue Origin, along with 75% of the mutually held Amazon shares, including voting power over MacKenzie's 25% stake.

Political Profile 23

Table 3.1 Beneficial Owners of Shares: Amazon Shareholders of March 2020

Name of Beneficial Owner	Amount and Nature of Beneficial Ownership	Percent of Class
Jeffrey P. Bezos	75,049,750[1]	15.1%
The Vanguard Group, Inc.	32,064,108	6.4%
BlackRock, Inc.	26,707,477	5.4%
Rosalind G. Brewer	190	*
Jamie S. Gorelick	6,405	*
Daniel P. Huttenlocher	950	*
Judith A. McGrath	2,324	*
Indra K. Nooyi	368	*
Jonathan J. Rubinstein	7,975	*
Thomas O. Ryder	9,319	*
Patricia Q. Stonesifer	6,845	*
Wendell P. Weeks	1,555	*
Brian T. Olsavsky	1,570	*
Jeffrey M. Blackburn	67,460	*
Andrew R. Jassy	100,540	*
Jeffrey A. Wilke	68,907	*
All directors and executive officers as a group (16 persons)	75,334,605	15.1%

*Less than 1%
(1) Includes 19,498,534 shares over which Bezos has sole voting power and no investment power.

Andrew Jassy, the CEO of Amazon Web Services (AWS), is Amazon's third-largest individual shareholder, with a reported 100,540 shares.[5] Jassy joined Amazon in 1997 and founded AWS in 2003. Since then, he has become one of the major leaders of Amazon's expansion in tech storage and cloud technology; crucially, he recognised that AWS could greatly increase the efficiency of Amazon's software engineers by storing and partly replicating the computing infrastructure for each project. The engineers felt "they were all reinventing the wheel on the infrastructure pieces and nothing they were building scaled beyond their own projects", Jassy recalls. AWS, which provides on-demand computing power in the cloud, helped fix that.[6]

Amazon's fourth-largest shareholder is Jeffrey Wilke, who owns 68,907 shares. Wilke joined Amazon in 1999 as its vice president and general manager, later serving as the senior vice president for the consumer business. He is now Amazon's CEO of Worldwide Consumer, a role he has held since April 2016. Wilke, whose background is in science, holds a Bachelor of Science, Engineering from Princeton University and completed graduate work at Massachusetts Institute of Technology's Leaders for Global Operations programme.

24 *Benedetta Brevini and Lukasz Swiatek*

Institutional investors together hold the majority ownership of Amazon through the 57.7% of the outstanding shares that they control, as shown in Table 3.1. The largest shareholders include Vanguard Group, Inc and Black-Rock, Inc, both major investment funds with worldwide interests.

Board of Directors and Interlocks

Amazon's Board of Directors is extremely revealing of the company's position as a digital communication giant. This also reflects the reality that, as demonstrated in Chapter 2 ("Economic Profile"), a growing percentage of Amazon's revenue comes from its investment in technology and, in particular, from AWS, which provides much of the government digital infrastructure in the U.S. and displays market dominance in terms of private businesses. Table 3.2 provides a snapshot of the board and the roles of its members, who are introduced in greater detail in this section.

Amazon has carefully recruited its board with an eye to sounding out its Silicon Valley competitors. Tom Alberg, who stepped down in 2019, created Madrona, which seeded both Amazon and many of its subsidiaries.[7] Alberg has also been significantly influential in private lobbying for autonomous vehicles in the Pacific Northwest, in addition to being a public proponent of quantum computing. Madrona's website promotes the firm's roles in the investment and development of the technology sector, primarily in the Pacific Northwest of the United States.[8] A number of companies listed within Madrona's portfolio either provide key services to Amazon or have since been acquired by Amazon. Alberg's skills are related specifically to

Table 3.2 Current Board of Directors, Amazon

Name	Audit Committee	Leadership Development and Compensation Committee	Nominating and Corporate Governance Committee
Jeffrey P. Bezos			
Rosalind G. Brewer		✓	
Jamie S. Gorelick			✓
Daniel P. Huttenlocher		✓	
Judith A. McGrath		✓	
Indra K. Nooyi	✓		
Jonathan J. Rubinstein			✓
Thomas O. Ryder	✓		
Patricia Q. Stonesifer			✓
Wendell P. Weeks	✓		

Source: Amazon

Political Profile 25

incubating and managing venture capital projects in the sphere of information and communication technologies.[9]

Jonathan Rubinstein (the former VP for Hewlett-Packard), Patricia Stonesifer (the former CEO of the Bill and Melinda Gates Foundation), and Wendell Weeks (the former CEO of Corning) have all brought insider knowledge from Silicon Valley. Daniel Huttenlocher came to Amazon's board from senior positions at MIT and Cornell University, as well as prominent technology commercialisation and research centres; he is currently the Dean of the MIT Schwarzman College of Computing.

A key appointment for Amazon's retail expansion was Rosalind Brewer, who came from Starbucks' executive team, having served as its COO (Group President of Americas) and a director since 2019. Previously, she served as the president and CEO of Sam's Club at the retail giant Walmart (from 2012 to 2017), again highlighting her crucial retail management experience.

Strong and close relations have been forged on both sides of U.S. politics, with Jamie Gorelick having been a close legal advisor to both of the Clintons in an official capacity, as well as an attorney for Jared Kushner, President Trump's son-in-law. Gorelick has been a director since February 2012. Amazon's official biography introduces her thus:

> Ms. Gorelick has been a partner with the law firm Wilmer Cutler Pickering Hale and Dorr LLP, a law firm in Washington D.C. since July 2003. She has held numerous positions in the U.S. government, serving as Deputy Attorney General of the United States and General Counsel of the Department of Defense.

Judith McGrath, a director since 2014, brings strategic media and communication industry experience. She also serves as a senior adviser to Astronauts Wanted: *No experience necessary. Previously, she served as the president of Astronauts Wanted (from 2013 to 2018) and the chair and CEO of MTV Networks Entertainment Group worldwide.

Finally, Jeff Bezos, the chairman of the Board of Directors, as well as the president and CEO of the corporation, is the linchpin of the board. In addition to being the founder of the aerospace company Blue Origin, Bezos is the owner of *The Washington Post*.

As discussed, the members of Amazon's Board of Directors also act as the directors of other organisations. These interlocking directorates – that is, individuals who are members of more than one organisational board – are just one part of other interorganisational relationships and communication dynamics, as Shumate et al.[10] point out. The three general reasons these authors provide for the existence of interlocking directorates apply to Amazon and its intricate relationships, which are typical of a consolidated

26 *Benedetta Brevini and Lukasz Swiatek*

corporation. First, drawing on the resource dependence view, interlocks may be used as a mechanism for collusion, monitoring, or co-optation: activities that are all designed to help control uncertain environments. As the previous section about ownership highlighted, Amazon operates in increasingly competitive and complex environments; consequently, the desire for some degree of control over such environments can be seen as a reason for the development of the interlocking directorate. Second, according to social class research, underlying social relations – typically taking the form of clubs and societies – foster both control and social cohesion among members of the elite, leading to interlocks. As the following sections about ties to the state and lobbying efforts will show, Amazon's leaders are part of wider elite networks. Today, it could be argued that interlocks also help in combatting digital feuds. Third, interlocks are formed because institutions seek legitimacy by obtaining board members from other organisations to enhance their stature in the eyes of stakeholders. As the final section in this chapter will illustrate, Amazon has particularly sought greater legitimacy in terms of ethnic and racial representation, leading to the appointment of more diverse leaders. These directors' membership on a wide variety of other boards of directors – in areas ranging from technology to food and beverages – highlights the diversity of the interlocking directorates at Amazon and reaffirms all three of the aforementioned key reasons for the existence of such interlocks.

Political Agenda

For many years, Amazon did not disclose its political posture. The corporation's stance on many issues was the subject of guesswork; few explicit answers were provided. Indeed, as Griswold[11] notes, Amazon's chief concern throughout most of its history had simply been "keeping customers happy and profit-hungry investors at bay". Inquiries about the organisation's political posture were particularly quieted in 2017. That year, at its annual shareholder meeting in Seattle, Bezos was asked a range of politically oriented questions; he responded to them by stating: "It's very important that Amazon, in my opinion, not oppose or favour any presidential candidate or elected official, that's not our job. Instead, the right thing for us is to take a very measured issue-by-issue approach."[12] He added that Amazon's employees would always, naturally, have their own stances on political issues and that the organisation would occasionally make its positions known; however, he cautioned: "When we take a stance on a particular issue it should be because it has an impact on the company or our employees". Although Amazon would continue to engage with all levels of government, Levy[13] summarised, it would not take public positions on many issues.

Political Profile 27

One of the rare instances in which Amazon voiced its political views involved a protest against a travel ban that had been imposed by President Donald Trump. Although the protest was cloaked in a discourse of equal opportunity, it ultimately served to benefit the organisation and its own employees. The impetus for the protest had been the president's executive order, issued on January 27, 2017, that temporarily banned individuals from seven predominantly Muslim countries – Iran, Iraq, Libya, Somalia, Sudan, Syria, and Yemen – from entering the U.S. for 90 days, and refugees from crossing U.S. borders for 120 days. In response, Washington's Attorney-General, Bob Ferguson, filed a lawsuit to block the executive order; Amazon was one of the many technology giants that filed a declaration of support for that lawsuit. Bezos[14] sent an email update about the situation to Amazon's employees, stating:

> We're a nation of immigrants whose diverse backgrounds, ideas, and points of view have helped us build and invent as a nation for over 240 years. No nation is better at harnessing the energies and talents of immigrants. It's a distinctive competitive advantage for our country – one we should not weaken.

In closing the email, he added: "To our employees in the U.S. and around the world who may be directly affected by this order, I want you to know that the full extent of Amazon's resources are behind you". The email's discourse of equal opportunity camouflaged the real intent of the declaration of support for the lawsuit: protecting Amazon's corporate interests. This is more plainly evident in an email sent by Beth Galetti, Amazon's Senior Vice President of Human Resources, to the company's employees. In her missive, Galetti[15] stated:

> From the very beginning, Amazon has been committed to equal rights, tolerance and diversity – and we always will be. As we've grown the company, we've worked hard to attract talented people from all over the world, and we believe this is one of the things that makes Amazon great – a diverse workforce helps us build better products for customers.

These comments not only emphasise a focus on the corporation's success; they reveal a focus on continuous growth: a pivotal aspect of Amazon's ideology (as the next chapter discusses) that has also propelled the expansion of its media and communication offerings.

Some communities in the United States had also highlighted Amazon's quiet liberal stance on various issues, particularly abortion. In particular, 2nd Vote – a right-wing activist group that investigates and then releases details

28 *Benedetta Brevini and Lukasz Swiatek*

of the ways in which consumer spending and organisational donations fund liberal organisations[16] – made light of the corporate behemoth's alleged pro-abortion spending patterns. In an analysis of retailers that it recommended shoppers avoid during the 2018 Christmas season, 2nd Vote[17] commented that: "Amazon directly funds the Population Council, an organization that targets impoverished areas for abortion". It recommended an alternative retailer. Earlier that year, Amazon removed the pro-life organisation Alliance Defending Freedom from its list of charities approved to participate in the AmazonSmile programme.[18] Pro-life commentators such as Lamb[19] queried the decision, as well as its reliance on the recommendation of the Southern Poverty Law Center (SPLC), which Amazon used to help it vet charities, even though other national organisations, such as the Department of Defense and the FBI, had stopped relying on it. The inconspicuousness of Amazon's actions in this area also relates to the U.S. political climate surrounding abortion. Green, Sakoui, and Newkirk[20] point out that major, liberal-leaning companies – among them Amazon – are loath to speak out in that area, as it is too politically sensitive.

The speculation about Amazon's general political stance ended in late 2019, when the corporation broke its self-imposed silence by publishing a webpage titled "Our Positions" on its *About Amazon* site. The webpage explicitly details many of the organisation's views and practices. The outline was published following criticisms of the Trump administration made by Amazon's Senior Vice President of Global Corporate Affairs, Jay Carney. The day before the webpage was published, Carney, the former press secretary to president Barack Obama, questioned the patriotism and credibility of the Trump White House, in addition to remarking that the president had violated longstanding American political norms, including commenting on the work of the Federal Reserve. Observers (such as Fung[21]) have noted that Trump has been a longstanding critic of Amazon and that tensions between his administration and the company were likely to increase following Carney's comments and the publication of the outline of its positions. At least the tensions accurately reflect the second statement prefacing the outline, which asserts that although the corporation's positions "are carefully considered and deeply held, there is much room for healthy debate and differing opinions".[22] The corporation will undoubtedly continue to attract both in the years to come.

Four of Amazon's 11 views, outlined by the webpage, relate to social issues. The first view presents the organisation's belief that the U.S. federal minimum wage ($7.25) is too low and argues that it should be raised in order to ameliorate the lives of millions of individuals. (Amazon is quick to point out that it pays a minimum wage of $15 an hour to all of its U.S.-based seasonal, temporary, part-time, and full-time workers.) In the fourth

Political Profile   29

position on the webpage, it states that diversity and inclusion are not just good for business; they are "simply right". The corporation considers it crucial to have diverse employees, foster a workplace culture that normalises inclusion, and help underrepresented groups enter the technology workforce. The fifth view emphasises that LGBTQ+ rights must be protected. In addition to mentioning its "early and strong" commitment to marriage equality, the organisation notes that it provides gender transition benefits and has received a perfect score on the Human Rights Campaign Foundation's Corporate Equality Index for three years running. Similarly, in the sixth position, Amazon emphasises its support for immigration reform and immigrants' rights. It argues that the U.S. should welcome the world's best and the brightest, and points out that 300,000 employees from different backgrounds number among its ranks.

Four positions relate to technology in different ways. In the third position presented on the webpage, the corporation holds that the energy industry is entitled to the same technologies as other industries. To that end, Amazon states (unsurprisingly) that it will continue to help businesses in the energy industry become more eco-friendly by providing them with cloud services. The seventh view presents the organisation's belief that all levels of government should have access to the best technology – including machine learning and "cloud" technologies – in order to ensure everyone's safety and security; the corporation affirms (also unsurprisingly) that it will continue to provide such advanced technology, particularly for the U.S. government and law enforcement agencies. The eighth position is a call to action rather than a position; it urges governments to enact a regulatory framework for facial recognition technology. In promoting its Amazon Rekognition tool, the organisation highlights the fact that this technology can be misused; as such, it exhorts governments to implement regulation to protect individuals' rights through the technology's transparent use. In its tenth view, it states its belief that U.S. federal law should protect consumer data privacy. In claiming that it has always followed privacy-by-design principles, the organisation comments that it also supports U.S. federal privacy legislation that "requires transparency, access to one's own personal information, ability to delete personal information, and that prohibits the sale of personal data without consent".

The final three positions relate to high-level action. In the second of the 11 positions, the corporation asserts that climate change is "real, serious, and action is needed from the public and private sectors". In addition to detailing some of its efforts in the area of sustainability, Amazon emphasises the international scientific consensus about human activities generating climate-warming trends. In the ninth view, the corporation contends that counterfeiters who sell their products in-person and online should face

30 Benedetta Brevini and Lukasz Swiatek

stronger penalties. Its justification for this stance is the harm caused to both retailers (particularly itself, of course) and consumers by the sale of counterfeit goods. Finally, it asserts that corporate tax codes around the world should incentivise job creation and investment in the economy. Tax codes between countries should be coordinated, it argues, to prevent both loopholes (that lead to artificially lower tax rates) and overlaps (that result in higher tax rates or redundant taxes).[23] Although all of these 11 positions do not explicitly mention Amazon's media and communication offerings, they all implicitly reflect, or impact, the development, production, distribution, and consumption dynamics of those offerings.

These positions ostensibly present the corporation as a forward-looking, socially responsible actor; however, viewed more critically, they are a series of either self-serving appeals (mainly to governments) to further its own ambitions, or reputationally restorative responses to the many criticisms that have been levelled at it over time. In this respect, the webpage and its positions squarely represent the communication component of Doorley and Garcia's[24] reputation formula (expressed as: "Reputation = Sum of Images = Performance + Behavior + Communication"). Normally, the three fundamental components of the formula (performance, behaviour, and communication) should reinforce each other, leading to a strong sum of images of an organisation in publics' minds, and thus to a strong reputation; in this instance, however, Amazon has strengthened its communication to try to offset weaknesses (both perceived and proven) in its performance and behaviour. Greene's[25] analysis of this ersatz "manifesto" lays bare these weaknesses. For example, the position on taxes, he points out, does not actually address the frequently made criticism that the corporation pays too little tax; the position on facial recognition technology overlooks the fact that the Rekognition tool has been sold to law enforcement agencies, which could wrongfully arrest innocent individuals as a result of weak or inaccurate evidence; and the positions on climate change and technology for the energy industry ignore the reproaches of critics (including its own employees, especially the Amazon Employees for Climate Justice group) that "cloud" computing helps energy companies accelerate oil and gas extraction.

Indirect Ties to the State

Although Amazon does not have direct ties to the state – and, indeed, has been criticised numerous times by the U.S. government – it does have indirect ties that it, and its founder, have attempted to strengthen over the years. In 2015, the corporation hired Jay Carney, a former White House press secretary for the Obama administration. As Amazon's Senior Vice President of

Political Profile 31

Global Corporate Affairs, Carney has substantially bolstered the corporation's political ties to Washington.[26] He has been particularly instrumental in augmenting its public policy and lobbying activities, which the remainder of this section discusses. The organisation's indirect ties to the state were also strengthened by its owner's purchase of *The Washington Post* in 2013. Bezos's acquisition was viewed as an attempt at challenging the intensifying unease in the capital city about the growing clout of the country's largest technology companies. In discussing the purchase of the newspaper, Shephard[27] observes that:

> Despite what Trump has suggested, there is no evidence that he [Bezos] is influencing its editorial direction – it has, in fact, done admirable work on Amazon. But the *Post* was not purchased because Bezos believes in civic engagement – it was purchased as part of a concerted effort to grow his company's influence in the capital.

Bezos's politically oriented activities in Washington have also increased through actions such as political donations (discussed elsewhere in this section) and his $12 million renovation of his $23 million Washington, D.C., mansion. As Griswold[28] argues, the company and its founder have become more and more "wary of Washington".

This growing wariness of government has led the corporation to engage in increasingly extensive and intensive lobbying over time, especially in the capital city. Around 2010, just two of Amazon's registered lobbyists were based in the capital. At the time, Romm[29] notes that federal regulators "fawned" over America's media giants (including Facebook and Google), "seeking a chance to associate themselves with companies considered to be engines of American economic recovery – and executives who could help pad their reelection coffers". The corporations were celebrated for being "great stories of American success", and their founders' noble-sounding remarks about corporate plans were given little scrutiny.[30] This situation changed half a decade later, when the companies found themselves being intensively criticised for issues such as privacy breaches, tax avoidance, antitrust, and environmental damage. The weaponisation of social media by the Russian government during the 2016 election campaign particularly unsettled lawmakers; afterwards, Congress began to subject the digital giants and their leaders to stronger public scrutiny. Interest increased in these corporations' growing lobbying activities, as well as the individuals appointed to lead them. Amazon, as mentioned previously, hired the former Obama administration press secretary Jay Carney in 2015; Facebook hired George W. Bush's White House Deputy Chief of Staff Joel Kaplan in 2011 to be its vice president of global public policy; in 2014, Uber appointed

32 Benedetta Brevini and Lukasz Swiatek

Obama's campaign manager David Plouffe as its senior vice president of policy and strategy; in 2018, Google enticed Karan Bhatia (who had held senior positions in the Bush administration, most notably as the Deputy U.S. Trade Representative) away from the General Electric conglomerate.[31] Interest in these individuals' and their teams' actions continued to grow, and details would occasionally be released. For instance, Amazon memorably provided clues in its response to the 2017 travel ban issued by President Trump. Drawing on Goffman,[32] the organisation provided a rare glimpse backstage, beyond its frontstage. In an email to employees, Bezos[33] revealed that: "Our public policy team in D.C. has reached out to senior administration officials to make our opposition clear. We've also reached out to congressional leaders on both sides of the aisle to explore legislative options", adding that the corporation was "working other legal options as well".

More recently, a fuller understanding of Amazon's growing lobbying efforts has emerged. The corporation adopted a more serious attitude towards these efforts in the final years of the Obama administration, with Newcomer[34] noting that its goal at the time involved shaping policy on matters such as regulations impacting delivery drones and state sales taxes. The hiring of Jay Carney marked a pivotal moment in the escalation of its lobbying activities. To entice the former White House press secretary into Amazon's fold, Bezos created the high-level post of Senior Vice President of Global Corporate Affairs, allowing Carney to run both public relations and public policy. In many respects, the action was logical, as these two areas are intertwined; lobbying (as a function of government relations management) is regarded as a central activity of public relations that enables government officials to engage in dialogue with multiple groups, as well as obtain information that will lead to more robust policy decisions and laws.[35] After Carney arrived, the corporation's policy division steadily expanded; a team with a few dozen employees now numbers around 250. Its status also changed within the organisational hierarchy. Previously, the policy team reported to the legal division and was two levels removed from Bezos and the organisation's senior executive group; it now reports to Carney, who is a member of that group. Also reporting to him are roughly 500 public relations and communications staff, bringing the total number of reports to approximately 800 worldwide.[36]

Some of Amazon's new hires are well-known individuals who have been strategically chosen to help the corporation achieve its lobbying goals in particular spheres. Nix[37] observes that these new employees consist of "well-connected government lawyers and congressional aides". One prominent example is Bryson Bachman, who formerly served as a senior counsel to the U.S. Department of Justice's Assistant Attorney-General for the Antitrust Division, Makan Delrahim. Ironically, in that role, Bachman assisted

Political Profile 33

in civil investigations, with a focus on vertical mergers; beforehand, he had been a trial attorney, contributing to the Antitrust Division's successful merger litigations against Anthem/Cigna and General Electric/Electrolux.[38] Amazon has also made a number of strategic high-profile diversity hires, including:

- Troy Clair (appointed as a Senior Manager for Public Policy), given his experience as the former chief of staff for Congressman G. K. Butterfield of North Carolina, who, in turn, was a former chairman of the Congressional Black Caucus;
- LaDavia Drane (also hired as a Senior Manager for Public Policy), owing to her position as a former staff chief for Congresswoman Yvette Clarke, who was a Congressional Black Caucus member;
- Rosalind Brewer (as a board member), owing to her high-profile status as the COO and group president for Starbucks; and
- Indra Nooyi (also as a board member), given her experience as the former chairwoman of PepsiCo.

Nix[39] adds that the first three of these hires were made due to the fact that numerous House of Representatives committees – including those on technology, government oversight, homeland security, financial services, and education – were chaired by black Democrats, making it vital for Amazon to have "a stable of minority lobbyists".

The corporation has also publicly acknowledged some of its lobbying activities. For instance, its positions webpage explicitly states that: "We support and lobby for immigration reform, including a legal pathway to citizenship for Dreamers and reforms to the green card and high-skilled visa programs, as well as actively participating in legal challenges to the travel ban", and "We are using our position as one of the nation's largest employers to encourage other companies to raise their wages and to lobby members of Congress and state legislatures to raise the minimum wage", as well as "Amazon supports and lobbies for U.S. federal policies that make intellectual property violations crimes with meaningful penalties, and for law enforcement to have resources to appropriately prosecute these crimes".[40] Additionally, the performance of each member of the policy team is monitored through the rigorous internal "Watering the Flowers" programme. As Kim[41] explains:

> The flowers represent elected officials, and the goal is to create a well-tended "garden" of pro-Amazon policymakers, from state governors and senators down to local officials and economic development teams, according to current and former employees. Based on sales management

34 *Benedetta Brevini and Lukasz Swiatek*

software from Salesforce, the program measures employees on things like how many meetings and events they attend with power players.

At its simplest level, the programme is emblematic of Amazon's increasing use of data to serve its own corporate ends; at a more complex level, it illustrates the organisation's exacting data-based monitoring of its workers – discussed in further detail in a later section – as part of a broader, intensifying, hyper-competitive culture in the U.S.[42]

Ever-larger sums of money are being spent by the corporation to undertake lobbying efforts. In 2017, it devoted $12.8 million to these activities. In 2018, it expended $14.2 million on them; that year, too, federal records showed that Amazon had "lobbied more government entities than any other tech company . . . and sought to exert its influence over more issues than any of its tech peers except Alphabet Inc.'s Google".[43] In 2019, it broke its own record by spending over $16 million on lobbying; Romm[44] calculates that this brought the corporation's expenditure in this area to a total of $80 million over ten years. Amazon is not unique among the digital media giants in its growing lobbying expenditure; the other giants have also been spending heavily in this area. Seven tech giants – led by Google, Facebook, and Amazon – are responsible for nearly half a billion dollars in lobbying expenditure over the past ten years; these giants now spend as much as, or more than, the banking, pharmaceutical, and oil giants, with Romm also noting that they have become "some of the most potent political forces" in Washington. Through their lobbying efforts, the corporations have sought not only to stave off tougher regulation, but also to increase their profits. Table 3.3 shows the most recent annual lobbying expenditure of the technology giants. It is worth noting that Facebook's total spending on federal lobbying over the past decade amounted to $81 million, while Google's total outlay for the same timeframe came to $150 million.[45]

Table 3.3 The Digital Giants' Spending on Lobbying in the U.S. in 2019[46]

Digital Giant	2019 U.S. Lobbying Expenditure
Facebook	$17 million
Amazon	$16 million
Google	$12 million
Microsoft	$10 million
Apple	$7 million
Uber	$2.3 million
Twitter	$1.48 million

Political Profile 35

Amazon's spending on lobbying activities has also been bolstered by Bezos's personal political expenditure. Until 2018, the charitable activities of the corporation's founder (and his partner) were reasonably modest; according to U.S. Federal Election Commission data,[47] Jeff and MacKenzie Bezos had given a total of $52,600 to federal candidates between 2007 to 2018, with $21,600 going to Republicans and $31,000 being given to Democrats. In 2018, they made what has been widely seen as Jeff's first major active foray into political financing: a $10 million contribution to the organisation With Honor, a nonpartisan Super Political Action Committee (PAC) that helps elect military veterans to U.S. Congress. While some[48] have seen the donation as a politically neutral gesture, it can be interpreted as a highly strategic move designed to influence the maximum number of political candidates. This latter interpretation was also made of Amazon's Political Action Committee's (Amazon PAC's) donations to Democrats and Republicans; in noting that the corporation is trying to "influence lawmakers across the spectrum", Kim[49] highlights the fact that the Amazon PAC spent $1.8 million in 2018: three times the amount that it spent in 2016. The PAC is funded only by voluntary contributions from the corporation's employees and shareholders. For this reason, the company has encouraged its stakeholders to make donations. Jeff Wilke, Amazon's CEO of Worldwide Consumer, encouraged staff to "join our effort to create a pro-customer public policy environment" in an email[50] sent to mark the launch of the "Amazon PAC 2019 membership campaign". In the email, he also explained that:

> We continue to face new legislative challenges and opportunities as our business continues to expand into new areas and the federal political environment changes in Washington, DC. Strong public policy advocacy allows us to continue to innovate on behalf of our customers, employees, and the many authors, artisans, and small businesses that sell in our stores. Our Amazon Political Action Committee (PAC) is an important component of that advocacy in the U.S.

This missive, similar to the staff email addressing the travel ban imposed by President Trump, disguises the real intent of the corporation's actions: protecting its bottom line and further opportunities for its expansion.

To enhance the impact of these lobbying activities and political donations, the dominant technology corporations' leaders have actively tried to build stronger personal relationships with key government figures. Bezos, unsurprisingly, has led Amazon's efforts in this area. The organisation's owner has participated in significant gatherings, large and small, with the

36 *Benedetta Brevini and Lukasz Swiatek*

following recount illustrating his varied networking schedule between late 2018 and early 2019.

> In September he roused an audience at the Economic Club of Washington with jokes and commentary about Trump and the role of the *Post* in a democracy. In late January he attended an 8 a.m. breakfast at the invitation of Don Graham, the former *Washington Post* owner, to hear billionaire investor Warren Buffett and former Federal Reserve chief Alan Greenspan talk about markets and the economy. The day before, he'd entertained guests at the exclusive Alfalfa Club dinner, an invitation-only, black-tie soiree for politicians, diplomats, and corporate executives. Buffett and Greenspan were both there.[51]

The other digital giants have engaged in similar strategic relationship-building. For instance, Apple has forged significant ties with the White House; Tim Cook, its CEO, has famously made friends with Donald Trump and his family. The connections being established – or, in many cases, strengthened – between these business and government leaders testify to the dynamism of the modern "power elite"; the members of this elite – that is, the members of America's top social stratum, including Bezos – know each other and enjoy the most power, money, and prestige: all of which are cumulative.[52] At Amazon, it is not just Bezos who is emblematic of the power elite. Jay Carney, for example, retains his close Washington insider connections; his wife, Claire Shipman, is a well-known television journalist, currently the senior national correspondent for ABC's *Good Morning America*; their son is the lead singer for the band Twenty20, which features three other children of former White House staff members.[53]

Amazon's increasing efforts on multiple fronts to influence the political landscape have yielded mixed results, revealing the corporation's limitations in being able to achieve its goals and create an environment conducive to its continual expansion. To date, it has claimed some victories, such as avoiding a regulatory challenge to its $13 billion acquisition of Whole Foods, securing job-creating deals to construct fulfilment centres, influencing music licensing regulations that serve streaming services including Amazon Music, and receiving approval (from the U.S. Department of Agriculture) to offer its Amazon Fresh grocery delivery service to food stamp recipients.[54] At the same time, it has been dealt a range of blows. Federal legislators – both Democrat and Republican – have brought a range of bills before Congress that aim to tighten the regulations for Amazon and other digital giants around online political advertising, the use of data, penalties for breaches of privacy, and accountability for problematic or dangerous content in users' posts.[55] Also, perhaps most significantly, Amazon lost a $10 billion Department of Defense bid to win a contract for the construction of a cloud computing system called JEDI; not only did Microsoft win the contract, but the Department faced a lawsuit for establishing a bidding process that only Amazon was able to win. Additionally, its preferred candidates in the local elections for the Seattle City Council failed to capture control of the local legislature, despite $1.5 million having been spent by the corporation on the campaign. The longstanding unpleasantness between Jeff Bezos and Donald Trump, who regularly ridicules Amazon and its founder, has also been a source of frustration for the organisation.[56]

Major Labour Controversies

To keep Amazon running – and to deliver its media- and communication-related products and services (among many others) – a vast workforce is required. In 2019, the corporation counted over 750,000 employees around the globe.[57] That year alone, it hired 96,700 people in three months; this jump in staff numbers – the biggest in the organisation's history – was due to the launch of its one-day Prime Delivery service that speeds up shipping. In order to ensure the success of this same-day delivery programme, apart from hiring extensively in the areas of transportation and order fulfilment, Amazon has been particularly augmenting the numbers of its employees in software engineering, sales, and marketing, in addition to hiring rapidly in video, devices, and international expansion.[58] At the time of writing, the corporation lists just over 39,000 vacancies on its *Amazon Jobs* portal.[59] Although the organisation says that it seeks "top talent from all industries and a range of backgrounds",[60] it also acknowledges that there are gaps in the types of individuals it hires; specifically, it admits that it needs to build a more diverse workforce, saying: "We have made year-over-year progress, but continue to strive for better representation across our various businesses".[61] A quick glance at its self-published global gender and U.S. race and ethnicity data – as of December 31, 2019 – shows why the company is so acutely aware of its shortcomings in this area. According to this data, women globally make up 42.7% of the organisation's workforce, while men make up 57.3%. Of its managers around the world, just 27.5% are women, while 72.5% are men. In terms of U.S. race and ethnicity, the organisation has made strides in having a more diverse workforce generally. However, in terms of its U.S. managers specifically, it has quite some way to go in achieving greater racial and ethnic representation – and having a greater balance between white and non-white managers, in particular – as illustrated by Table 3.4.[62]

38 Benedetta Brevini and Lukasz Swiatek

Table 3.4 Race and Ethnicity Among Amazon's U.S. Managers and Non-managerial Employees[63]

Race and Ethnicity (Type)	U.S. Non-managerial Staff	U.S. Managers
White	34.7%	59.3%
Black/African American	26.5%	8.3%
Asian	15.4%	20.8%
Hispanic/Latinx	18.5%	8.1%
Native American	1.3%	0.6%
Two or more races	3.6%	3.0%

Amazon's treatment of its employees has been a focus of intense scrutiny for many years. A memorable 2015 exposé by *The New York Times* discovered an unforgiving workplace whose employees were pushed to work 80 hours a week, stay online constantly (even during the night to reply to messages), meet overly high standards, openly criticise co-workers' ideas in meetings, and send secret feedback to those co-workers' managers.[64] While this white-collar part of the organisation was accurately described by the newspaper's article as "bruising", it is the blue-collar end of the organisation that has undoubtedly weathered more storms. The numerous testimonies of frontline employees paint a bleaker picture of working life within the corporation. Amazon's U.S. warehouse employees[65,66,67] have repeatedly voiced complaints about overly short on-shift breaks, injury rates that are higher than the national average, unaddressed safety concerns, stress-inducing unreasonable work targets that are closely monitored electronically, an exhausting pace of work (due to these targets), and work-induced chronic physical pains. Reports from other countries have portrayed a similar negative picture of harsh frontline working conditions. In Australia, for instance, the corporation's warehouse staff[68] have spoken of a workplace culture built around fear, a system of being sent home early when orders are completed (and not being paid for the remainder of the day's shift), as well as high-pressure targets that force workers sometimes to take safety shortcuts and skip toilet breaks. The inability to take proper breaks was also identified as a major issue in the UK, where investigative reporting found that some workers were having to urinate into bottles to avoid going to the toilet in order to meet package-processing targets; reports also found that some workers were routinely falling asleep on the job as a result of the intense workload and were being criticised for taking sick days.[69] Gershgorn et. al.[70] sum up these workers' testimonies by describing Amazon as a "ruthless workplace driven by the demand for productivity above all else". The corporation has always denied the claims made about its workplaces and, instead, highlighted its health-and-safety-focused policies and practices.

Political Profile 39

Criticisms of low pay rates have also been made repeatedly over the years and have prompted vigorous public relations responses from the corporation and its staff. Some of the most memorable of these responses followed attacks made by Senator Bernie Sanders, who criticised Amazon for low pay and inadequate benefits for its workers. The senator even introduced a bill titled Stop Bad Employers by Zeroing Out Subsidies Act – or the Stop BEZOS Act – to Congress in an effort to compel Amazon and other large corporations whose employees require federal benefits, such as food stamps and Medicaid, to contribute to the cost of those benefits. Amazon, making a rare response through a post on its blog, denounced the senator. Among other rebuttals, the company stated:

> In addition to highly competitive wages and a climate controlled, safe workplace, Amazon provides employees with a comprehensive benefit package including health insurance, disability insurance, retirement savings plans, and company stock. The company also offers up to 20 weeks of paid leave and innovative benefits such as LeaveShare and Ramp-Back, which give new parents flexibility with their growing families. With LeaveShare, employees share their Amazon paid leave with their spouse or domestic partner if their employer does not offer paid leave. RampBack gives new moms additional control over the pace at which they return to work. Just as with Amazon's health care plan, these benefits are egalitarian – they are the same for fulfillment center and customer service employees as they are for Amazon's most senior executives.[71]

In addition to this corporate apologia – that is, the company's response to criticisms and presentation of its competing account of its organisational actions[72] – Amazon undertook a public relations effort involving employees. Specifically, it encouraged employees to contact Senator Sanders and tell him about their (positive) experiences of working for the company.[73] Additionally, to counter the criticisms of hostile publics – that is, publics who collectively pose a reputational threat to an organisation by engaging in both negative online and word-of-mouth behaviours[74] – the corporation tasked specific fulfilment centre workers with the job of being Twitter "ambassadors". Over two weeks, 16 accounts from various "ambassadors" were reported to have opened; as Tynan[75] observed:

> The accounts are remarkably uniform in look and tone. All feature the familiar burnt-umber Amazon smile logo as their Twitter cover. All sport a photo of the account's owner posed inside a warehouse, though many of their faces are not visible, and a first name but not a last one. All are relentlessly upbeat and articulate.

40 *Benedetta Brevini and Lukasz Swiatek*

The ambassadors' posts noted that, among other things, employees are allowed to go to the toilet at any time, drink water while working, and enjoy working in well-lit spaces with large fans.[76]

The corporation's strongest response to the sustained criticisms of its inadequate benefits and pay rates has undoubtedly been its increase of the minimum wage for its U.S. and UK employees. In 2018, several weeks after Senator Sanders's attacks, it announced increases to $15 an hour for its U.S. workers (representing double the federal minimum wage), £10.50 an hour for London employees (representing a rise of 28% in comparison with the UK's minimum wage), and £9.50 for workers across the rest of the UK (representing a rise of 18%).[77] Additionally, the company announced that its public policy team would begin advocating for an increase to the U.S. federal minimum wage itself. The move was designed to appear as a benevolent corporate gesture before Christmas; Bezos, through an announcement on Amazon's blog,[78] stated: "We listened to our critics, thought hard about what we wanted to do, and decided we want to lead. . . . We're excited about this change and encourage our competitors and other large employers to join us". However, the reality of the increases in the minimum wages across both sides of the Atlantic was much more complex and represented less of a charitable action than a strategic, market-based move. As Elliott[79] observes, Amazon had simply been pressured simultaneously from two sources: first, major political figures (chief among them Donald Trump and Bernie Sanders in the U.S., and the GMB trade union and the Archbishop of Canterbury in the UK) and, second, a tightening labour market. Amazon had been continuing to struggle to fill vacancies. Elliott notes that: "In Britain and the US, unemployment is about 4%, meaning workers – even deunionised workers – have more freedom to change job if they are unhappy". In raising the minimum wages, Amazon also removed monthly bonuses and stock awards, explaining at the time that the raise "more than compensates" for the two other lost benefits; however, workers and news outlets calculated that, as a result, employees actually stood to make less money.[80]

The pressure exerted by workers – particularly those on Amazon's frontlines – has been crucial in bringing about changes to working conditions, especially during the COVID-19 pandemic. Warehouse staff criticised the company for failing to provide them with safe working conditions during the spread of the coronavirus disease. Although workers had been mobilising for some time in visible and vocal opposition to their treatment – by, for example, walking off the job, circulating public and private petitions, speaking with media representatives, and leading other campaigns[81] – the actions taken during the pandemic have been among the most successful, due to the workers' newly available leverage. As Greene[82] rightly notes, the

Political Profile 41

workers have been able to use to their advantage the twin facts that Amazon customers have been house-bound *en masse*, thus requiring delivered purchases more than ever, and that hiring new staff has been exceptionally difficult while restrictions, including population movement controls, have been in place. The corporation acquiesced to many of the workers' demands (including some longstanding pleas), partly also because it realised how significantly it had mishandled the spread of the virus by providing ineffective quarantine approaches, missing warnings from its workers, and firing a protest organiser for violating quarantine: a move that sparked significant backlash. Dzieza[83] notes just how significantly Amazon escalated its response within weeks of numerous protests and growing public scrutiny; by mid-March the corporation had announced that:

> employees could take unlimited time off without pay (previously, they would be fired for more than taking a certain amount), and they would receive up to two weeks of paid leave if they tested positive for COVID-19 or were placed in quarantine. Later, the company raised pay by $2 per hour, doubled overtime pay, and gave part-time workers paid time off. As the virus spread, Amazon moved warehouse break room tables apart, staggered shifts, canceled stand-up meetings, and made other adjustments to enable greater distance between workers.

It is not just frontline, blue-collar workers who have become more vocal. The corporation's white-collar staff have also more actively opposed its actions and policies on various fronts. Dissent from the professional parts of Amazon's workforce – over, for example, the corporation's role in aggravating climate change by funding climate change-denying lobbyists and politicians, as well as providing the cloud computing technology being used by oil- and gas-extracting companies – is unique in many ways, owing to the corporation's investment in the professionals and their skills, as well the difficulty in replacing them.[84]

Workers' jobs and conditions may be further impacted in the coming years by the advancement of robotic technologies and their ever-deeper integration into Amazon's existing systems. One of the corporation's divisions, Amazon Robotics (formerly Kiva Systems), has been manufacturing mobile robotic fulfilment systems since 2012, having previously provided these systems for other companies, including Walgreens and Office Depot. The robotic systems – including small drive units and robotic arms – are designed to help Amazon process orders more effectively and efficiently, as well as enhance safety in fulfilment centres; the net result, the corporation claims, is the ability to "deliver a smarter, faster, more consistent customer experience".[85] However, the increasing integration of robotic technologies

42 Benedetta Brevini and Lukasz Swiatek

is likely to yield decidedly mixed results in the coming years. Indeed, Del Rey[86] has argued that it will have a "seismic" impact on the warehouse industry, due to the automation of jobs previously undertaken by humans; by his estimates, the rise of artificially intelligent robots will lead to the replacement of nearly every humanly undertaken task. Datafication – that is, the process of transforming into data all of the numerous, previously unquantified aspects of our world[87] – has already proven controversial for the company, specifically in the use of technologies to track and terminate frontline workers for not meeting their productivity targets. According to the calculation in one investigative report, based on internal documents, the corporation terminates approximately 10% of its blue-collar workers each year for not moving packages through its warehouses quickly enough based on the calculations of tracking technologies.[88] Amazon has also drawn criticisms for its other technologies designed to increase efficiency, such as the crowdsourcing website Mechanical Turk: a crowd employment platform that allows labour to be sourced remotely. Amazon and the platform have been condemned for exploiting low-cost digital labour and not providing the appropriate social protections.[89] Criticisms of technologies that provide inadequate remuneration for individuals at best, and make jobs obsolete altogether at worst, will only grow; Amazon, like many other organisations, will need to consider carefully these technologies' broader and longer-term social and economic implications, which are still in the early stages of being charted.[90] Amazon is not only in a unique position to appraise technological developments carefully due to its leading position as a technology user and developer; it is also in an important position to do so, due to its existing labour-related issues and the continual growth of its workforces around the world.

Notes

1. U.S. Securities and Exchange Commission. (2020). AMAZON COM INC. www.sec.gov/cgi-bin/own-disp?action=getissuer&CIK=0001018724.
2. Capriel, J. (2020, February 11). Jeff Bezos has sold 18.5 million shares of Amazon in 10 years. Here's how much that stock was worth. *Washington Business Journal*. www.bizjournals.com/washington/news/2020/02/11/jeff-bezos-has-sold-18-5-million-shares-of-amazon.html.
3. Denning, S. (2018, September 19). Why Jeff Bezos bought The Washington Post. *Forbes*. www.forbes.com/sites/stephaniedenning/2018/09/19/why-jeff-bezos-bought-the-washington-post/#2096aace3aab.
4. Ponciano, J. (2020, April 18). These 10 billionaires gained $55 billion this week as retail and tech stocks surged. *Forbes*. www.forbes.com/sites/jonathan ponciano/2020/04/18/these-ten-billionaires-gained-55-billion-this-week-as-retail-and-tech-stocks-surged/#1dd82f415d23.
5. According to the 2020 Amazon Proxy statement.

Political Profile   43

6. Hook, L. (2016, March 18). Person of the year: Amazon Web Services' Andy Jassy. *Financial Times*. www.ft.com/content/a515eb7a-d0ef-11e5-831d-09f 7778e7377.
7. Madrona. (n.d.). Tom Alberg [profile]. www.madrona.com/team-profiles/tom-alberg/.
8. Madrona.(n.d.).Investmentthemesfor2019.www.madrona.com/madrona-invest ment-themes-for-2019/.
9. Amazon. (2018). Investor Proxy Statement 2018. https://ir.aboutamazon.com/ static-files/3af60b72-8be7-4dad-aef9-dd87b94a60f0.
10. Shumate, M., Atouba, Y., Cooper, K. R., & Pilny, A. (2017). Interorganizational communication. In C. R. Scott & L. Lewis (Eds.), *The international encyclopedia of organizational communication* (pp. 1–24). Chichester: Wiley-Blackwell. https://doi.org/10.1002/9781118955567.wbieoc117.
11. Griswold, A. (2018, September 8). Hating Amazon is one thing the hard left and hard right agree on. *Quartz*. https://qz.com/1380446/hating-amazon-is-one-thing-the-hard-left-and-hard-right-agree-on/.
12. Levy, N. (2017, May 23). Challenged at shareholder meeting, Jeff Bezos explains Amazon's political approach. *GeekWire*. www.geekwire.com/2017/ challenged-opposition-trump-travel-ban-amazons-bezos-explains-companys-political-approach/.
13. Ibid.
14. Stampher, J. (2017, January 30). Amazon CEO Jeff Bezos on Trump's immigration ban: "We're a nation of immigrants". *GeekWire*. www.geekwire. com/2017/amazon-ceo-jeff-bezos-says-company-not-support-trumps-immigra tion-ban-nation-immigrants/.
15. Ibid.
16. 2nd Vote. (2020). About 2ndVote. *2nd Vote*. www.2ndvote.com/about-2ndvote/.
17. Mainwaring, D. (2018, December 3). Where not to shop for Christmas: How consumers can align their dollars with their pro-life values. *Life Site News*. www. lifesitenews.com/news/where-not-to-shop-for-christmas-how-consumers-can-align-their-dollars-with.
18. Bilger, M. (2018). Amazon kicks pro-life organization out of AmazonSmile program. *Life News*. www.lifenews.com/2018/05/04/amazon-kicks-pro-life-organization-out-of-amazonsmile-program/.
19. Lamb, M. (2018). Amazon bans pro-life group from its approved list of charities in AmazonSmile. *Life News*. www.lifenews.com/2018/05/08/amazon-bans-pro-life-group-from-its-approved-list-of-charities-in-amazonsmile/.
20. Green, J., Sakoui, A., & Newkirk, M. (2019, May 19). Enter the abortion debate? Big companies can't see the upside. *Bloomberg*. www.bloomberg. com/news/articles/2019-05-19/enter-the-abortion-debate-big-companies-can-t-see-the-upside.
21. Fung, B. (2019, October 11). Amazon lays out its policies on political and social issues. *CNN Business*. https://edition.cnn.com/2019/10/10/tech/amazon-policy-positions-jay-carney/index.html.
22. Amazon. (2019a). Our positions. *About Amazon*. www.aboutamazon.com/ our-company/our-positions.
23. Ibid.
24. Doorley, J., & Garcia, H. F. (2015). Reputation management. In J. Doorley & H. F. Garcia (Eds.), *Reputation management: The key to successful public relations and corporate communication* (pp. 1–44). New York: Routledge.

25. Greene, J. (2019, October 11). Amazon policy manifesto responds to environmental, workplace and data-privacy critics. *The Washington Post.* www.washingtonpost.com/technology/2019/10/11/amazon-policy-manifesto-responds-environmental-workplace-data-privacy-critics/.
26. Wilson, M. (2015, February 26). Amazon hires Obama's former press secretary as a senior VP. *Chain Store Age.* https://chainstoreage.com/operations/amazon-hires-obamas-former-press-secretary-senior-vp.
27. Shephard, A. (2020, February 5). The Washington Post has gotten off easy for too long. *The New Republic.* https://newrepublic.com/article/156452/washington-post-gotten-off-easy-long.
28. Griswold (2018) op. cit.
29. Romm, T. (2020, January 23). Tech giants led by Amazon, Facebook and Google spent nearly half a billion on lobbying over the past decade, new data shows. *The Washington Post.* www.washingtonpost.com/technology/2020/01/22/amazon-facebook-google-lobbying-2019/.
30. Ibid.
31. Kim, E. (2019, June 28). Life after Obama: Jay Carney is a top advisor to Jeff Bezos and architect of Amazon's HQ2. *CNBC.* www.cnbc.com/2019/06/28/amazon-pr-and-policy-chief-jay-carney-gets-a-bigger-profile.html.
32. Goffman, E. (1959). *The presentation of self in everyday life.* New York: Doubleday.
33. Stampher (2017) op. cit.
34. Newcomer, E. (2019, November 19). Amazon pours record cash into lobbying, reaps little in return. *Bloomberg.* www.bloomberg.com/news/articles/2019-11-19/amazon-stumbles-in-attempts-to-play-politics.
35. Hobbs, M., & Swiatek, L. (2019). Public relations and lobbying: Influencing politics and policy. In M. Sheehan (Ed.), *Advocates and persuaders* (pp. 159–180). North Melbourne: Australian Scholarly Publishing.
36. Kim (2019) op. cit.
37. Nix, N. (2019, March 7). Amazon is flooding D.C. with money and muscle: The influence game. *Bloomberg Businessweek.* www.bloomberg.com/graphics/2019-amazon-lobbying/.
38. U.S. Department of Justice. (2018). *Division update spring 2018.* Washington: U.S. Department of Justice. www.justice.gov/atr/division-operations/division-update-spring-2018/meet-front-office.
39. Nix (2019) op. cit.
40. Amazon (2019a). op. cit.
41. Kim (2019) op. cit.
42. Heffernan, M. (2014). *A bigger prize: Why competition isn't everything & how we do better.* London: Simon & Schuster.
43. Nix (2019) op. cit.
44. Romm (2020) op. cit.
45. Ibid.
46. Ibid.
47. Epstein, R. J. (2018, September 5). Amazon founder Jeff Bezos gives $10 million to Super PAC in first major political contribution. *The Wall Street Journal.* www.wsj.com/articles/amazon-founder-jeff-bezos-gives-10-million-to-super-pac-in-first-major-political-contribution-1536141600.
48. Ibid.
49. Kim (2019) op. cit.

50. Ibid.
51. Nix (2019) op. cit.
52. Mills, C. W. (2000 [1956]). *The power elite*. New York: Oxford University Press.
53. Kim (2019) op. cit.
54. Newcomer (2019) op. cit.
55. Romm (2020) op. cit.
56. Newcomer (2019) op. cit.
57. Greene, J. (2020a, January 28). Amazon employees launch mass defiance of company communications policy in support of colleagues. *The Washington Post*. www.washingtonpost.com/technology/2020/01/26/amazon-employees-plan-mass-defiance-company-communications-policy-support-colleagues/.
58. Levy, N. (2019, October 24). Amazon tops 750,000 employees for the first time, adding nearly 100,000 people in three months. *GeekWire*. www.geek wire.com/2019/amazon-tops-750000-employees-first-time-adding-nearly-100000-people-three-months/.
59. Amazon. (2020a). Find jobs. *Amazon Jobs*. www.amazon.jobs/en.
60. Amazon. (2020b). Working at Amazon. *Amazon Jobs*. www.aboutamazon.com/working-at-amazon.
61. About Amazon Staff. (2020a). Our workforce data. *About Amazon*. www.about amazon.com/working-at-amazon/diversity-and-inclusion/our-workforce-data.
62. Ibid.
63. Ibid.
64. Kantor, J., & Streitfeld, D. (2015, August 15). Inside Amazon: Wrestling big ideas in a bruising workplace. *The New York Times*. www.nytimes.com/2015/08/16/technology/inside-amazon-wrestling-big-ideas-in-a-bruising-workplace.html.
65. Godlewski, N. (2018, December 9). Amazon working conditions: Urinating in trash cans, shamed to work injured, list of employee complaints. *Newsweek*. www.newsweek.com/amazon-drivers-warehouse-conditions-workers-com-plains-jeff-bezos-bernie-1118849.
66. Sainato, M. (2020, February 5). "I'm not a robot": Amazon workers condemn unsafe, grueling conditions at warehouse. *The Guardian*. www.theguard-ian.com/technology/2020/feb/05/amazon-workers-protest-unsafe-grueling-conditions-warehouse.
67. Spitznagel, E. (2019, July 13). Inside the hellish workday of an Amazon warehouse employee. *New York Post*. https://nypost.com/2019/07/13/inside-the-hellish-workday-of-an-amazon-warehouse-employee/.
68. Burin, M. (2019, February 27). "They resent the fact I'm not a robot". *ABC News*. www.abc.net.au/news/2019-02-27/amazon-australia-warehouse-working-conditions/10807308.
69. Bonazzo, J. (2018, April 16). Report: Amazon workers have to process 300 packages an hour and pee in bottles. *Observer*. https://observer.com/2018/04/amazon-britain-harsh-working-conditions/.
70. Gershgorn, D., Griswold, A., Murphy, M., Coren, M. J., & Kessler, S. (2017, August 20). What is Amazon, really? *Quartz*. https://qz.com/1051814/what-is-amazon-really/.
71. Day One Staff. (2018a, August 29). Response to Senator Sanders. *Day One: The Amazon Blog*. https://blog.aboutamazon.com/company-news/response-to-senator-sanders.

72. Hearit, K. M. (2001). Corporate apologia when an organization speaks in defense of itself. In R. L. Heath & G. Vasquez (Eds.), *Handbook of public relations* (pp. 501–511). Thousand Oaks, CA: Sage Publications.
73. Griswold (2018) op. cit.
74. Krishna, A., & Kim, S. (2016). Encouraging the rise of fan publics: Bridging strategy to understand fan publics' positive communicative actions. In A. L. Hutchins & N. T. J. Tindall (Eds.), *Public relations and participatory culture: Fandom, social media and community engagement* (pp. 21–32). Routledge.
75. Tynan, D. (2018, August 24). Amazon's "ambassador" workers assure Twitter: We can go to the toilet any time. *The Guardian.* www.theguardian.com/technology/2018/aug/23/amazon-fc-ambassadors-twitter-working-conditions.
76. Ibid.
77. Partington, R. (2018, October 2). Amazon raises minimum wage for US and UK employees. *The Guardian.* www.theguardian.com/technology/2018/oct/02/amazon-raises-minimum-wage-us-uk-employees.
78. Day One Staff. (2018b, October 2). Amazon raises minimum wage to $15 for all U.S. Employees. *Day One: The Amazon Blog.* https://blog.about amazon.com/working-at-amazon/amazon-raises-minimum-wage-to-15-for-all-us-employees.
79. Elliott, L. (2018, October 3). Even Amazon isn't immune to political and economic pressure. *The Guardian.* www.theguardian.com/technology/2018/oct/02/even-amazon-must-heed-laws-politics-and-economics.
80. Kim, E. (2018, October 3). Amazon's hourly workers lose monthly bonuses and stock awards as minimum wage increases. *CNBC.* www.cnbc.com/2018/10/03/amazon-hourly-workers-lose-monthly-bonuses-stock-awards.html.
81. Ghaffary, S. (2019, December 23). Amazon warehouse workers doing "back-breaking" work walked off the job in protest. *Vox.* www.vox.com/recode/2019/12/10/21005098/amazon-warehouse-workers-sacramento.
82. Greene, J. (2020b, April 9). Amazon needs its workers more than ever, giving them leverage to push for safer warehouses. *The Washington Post.* www.washingtonpost.com/technology/2020/04/09/amazon-workers-union-unrest/.
83. Dzieza, J. (2020, April 10). Warehouse workers are forcing Amazon to take COVID-19 seriously. *The Verge.* www.theverge.com/2020/4/10/21216172/amazon-coronavirus-protests-response-safety-jfk8-fired-covid-19.
84. Greene, J. (2020c, January 28). Amazon employees launch mass defiance of company communications policy in support of colleagues. *The Washington Post.* www.washingtonpost.com/technology/2020/01/26/amazon-employees-plan-mass-defiance-company-communications-policy-support-colleagues/.
85. About Amazon Staff. (2020b). What robots do (and don't do) at Amazon fulfillment centers. *About Amazon.* www.aboutamazon.com/amazon-fulfillment/our-innovation/what-robots-do-and-dont-do-at-amazon-fulfillment-centers/.
86. Del Rey, J. (2019, December 11). How robots are transforming Amazon warehouse jobs – for better and worse. *Vox.* www.vox.com/recode/2019/12/11/20982652/robots-amazon-warehouse-jobs-automation.
87. Cukier, K., & Mayer-Schoenberger, V. (2013). The rise of big data: How it's changing the way we think about the world. *Foreign Affairs*, 92. www.foreignaffairs.com/articles/2013-04-03/rise-big-data.
88. Lecher, C. (2019, April 25). How Amazon automatically tracks and fires warehouse workers for "productivity": Documents show how the company tracks

and terminates workers. *The Verge.* www.theverge.com/2019/4/25/18516004/amazon-warehouse-fulfillment-centers-productivity-firing-terminations.
89. Bergvall-Kåreborn, B., & Howcroft, D. (2014). Amazon Mechanical Turk and the commodification of labour. *New Technology, Work and Employment*, 29(3), 213–223. https://doi.org/10.1111/ntwe.12038.
90. Galloway, C., & Swiatek, L. (2018). Public relations and artificial intelligence: It's not (just) about robots. *Public Relations Review*, 44(5), pp. 734–740. http://dx.doi.org/10.1016/j.pubrev.2018.10.008.

4 Cultural Profile

Lukasz Swiatek

Amazon has become a significant actor in the global media landscape in no small part due to its cultural profile and the increasing integration of its media and communication offerings into everyday life. Indeed, its cultural profile as a driven and growing communication giant has enabled it to trade in more and more diversified media (its own and others). This chapter discusses the key aspects of this profile. It looks at the internal and external dimensions of the corporation's cultural profile in relation to everyday life, its ideology and symbolic universe, its most popular communication and media products and services, as well as the key parts of its community engagement.

Organisational Cultural Profile in Relation to Everyday Life

Amazon's rapid growth and diversification have been facilitated by its cultural profile. In this respect, Cameron and Quinn[1] provide a useful tool to understand an organisation's (internal) makeup. The authors' model presents four typical organisational cultural profiles: a clan culture, an adhocracy culture, a hierarchy culture, and a market culture. These four profiles are not mutually exclusive, and organisations' cultures typically fall largely within one primary culture and other, secondary cultures. Based on the research detailed across the previous chapters, Amazon displays elements of the hierarchy culture, due to the fact that it is largely a highly structured organisation; its leaders are efficiency-minded; its success is defined in terms of low cost, dependable delivery and smooth scheduling; and one of its key long-term concerns is ensuring efficient, smooth operations. It also displays elements of the adhocracy culture, as it exhibits entrepreneurialism and creativity (especially among its professional or white-collar staff), undertakes a substantial amount of innovation, and provides new services and products. However, as the data in this book has already highlighted, it

Cultural Profile   49

undoubtedly embodies a market culture above all. This is due to the fact that it is a results-oriented organisation whose long-term focus is on competitive activity and the achievement of measurable goals and targets. Its success is defined by penetration and market share, with competitive pricing and market leadership also being important; additionally, its leaders are "hard drivers, producers, and competitors".[2] This cultural profile has made Amazon a popular and innovative organisation, on the one hand, and led to significant challenges (as the previous chapters have discussed) on the other hand.

The corporation has also embedded itself, as well as its products and services, more and more undetectably into individuals' everyday lives. It has brought into its purview both the ordinary and the extraordinary: the mundane artefacts on which modern existence relies (such as household products) and the non-routine items (such as high-end entertainment) that can only be developed and delivered by specialists. In this respect, Quinn[3] rightly points out that Amazon deliberately:

> wants to fade from your life without ever leaving it. It wants to reduce all the friction from commerce. It wants you to walk around your home and tell Alexa what you want. It wants you to simply press a button by your washing machine when you're low on detergent. It wants its couriers to stealthily leave packages in your home when you're not there. It wants you to walk into a store, take what you need and leave. It wants to send you things you didn't even know you needed. It revolutionized online shopping with one-click checkout and two-day delivery. Next is no click and nearly instantaneous. There's no backlash if there's nothing to really think about.

In this way, the corporation both draws from, and contributes to, the modern "impulse society",[4] which is marked by continuous searches for short-term pleasure, increasing discretionary consumption (instead of the autonomous consumption of necessary goods and services), and superabundant entertainment. One of the key mechanisms that has allowed Amazon to feed modern impulses so effectively has been its delivery model. Speedy deliveries following comfortable at-home shopping have made the fulfilment of customers' desires easier and easier; such convenient service is also, McFadden[5] points out, a major reason why the corporation's popularity has continued to grow so rapidly. Other reasons include innovations that customers believe have made their lives easier, such as recommended products based on previous searches, and the inclusion of customer reviews of products.

All of these internal and external dimensions of the corporation's cultural profile have led it to become indispensable for scores of individuals in the U.S. and around the world. These individuals have come to rely on many

50   *Lukasz Swiatek*

of Amazon's different offerings, among them its media and communication products and services. This reliance partly stems from broader socio-economic factors that increasingly affect individuals: overwork, a lack of time, and the growing cost of living; Willis-Aronowitz[6] quips that "[y]ou have to be an able-bodied person with remarkable affluence and free time" to avoid having to make use of Amazon. The reliance also partly comes from the way in which the corporation has structured its offerings; the most conspicuous example in this regard is the Amazon Prime service, which provides one- to two-day shipping for a fixed annual price (currently $119 per year, increased from its 2014 price of $99, and increased previously from its original price of $79). Bezos assumed customers' willingness to pay for the frictionless expedited service, and he was proven correct. Prime has not only netted the corporation billions of dollars in revenue; it has also become "indispensable" for millions of users.[7] The shipping service is a salient example of the way in which the corporation has brought its ideology to life in nurturing individuals' growing dependence on it and its offerings.

Ideology and Symbolic Universe

Understanding Amazon's ideology is vital to understanding how it became the corporate juggernaut it is today, continuing to provide an increasingly diverse suite of products and services, not least in terms of communication and media. Intensity and continuity are the core pair of ideas linked to the group; this twofold ideology has been transmitted by the corporation to its publics, both internal and external, in various ways over the years. However, aspects of this ideology are flawed, as are all hegemonic ideologies conveyed by dominant groups to others through various forms of media.[8] The previous chapters in this book have already demonstrated many of the issues that have arisen for Amazon as a result of the propagation of its ideology. The root of these ideas, in many ways, is Jeff Bezos's conceptualisation of his business as a flywheel. This spinning device – most often found in engines, and designed to store rotational energy efficiently – epitomised for Bezos how his corporation should be run. As Gershgorn et. al.[9] explain:

> Amazon CEO Jeff Bezos borrowed the term from business consultant Jim Collins back in the early days of Amazon. It describes a cycle in which a company cuts prices to attract customers, which increases sales and attracts more customers, which allows the company to benefit from economies of scale (bundling together logistics and other routine costs), until, ultimately, the company can cut prices again, spinning the flywheel anew. The flywheel is the best encapsulation of Amazon's

Cultural Profile 51

dual ambitions: to be customer-obsessed, and to conquer the modern commercial world.

The authors also point out that this idea is not just a foundational metaphor that is now gathering dust; the flywheel informs every business decision that Amazon makes. The continuous intensity that drives the corporation was also reflected in the original name – Relentless – that Bezos chose for it at one point. The web address relentless.com was even registered initially; it is still live and redirects visitors to the amazon.com website. Amazon – named, apparently, after Bezos thumbed through a dictionary, liked the connotation offered by the world's largest river, and realised that a name beginning with the letter A would sit at the top of alphabetised lists – is undoubtedly a much more agreeable name; however, as *The Economist* has pointed out, if Relentless was "a little lacking in touchy-feeliness, it captured the ambition nicely".[10] Another potential name that was initially considered for the corporation was Cadabra (from the word abracadabra), suggesting magic.[11] It was abandoned, though, after Bezos realised that it could be misheard as the word cadaver. Nevertheless, the appeal to magic is also indicative of the illusory nature of the dominant ideas at the heart of the corporation.

No discussion of Amazon's ideology would be complete without a consideration of the capitalist system that not only drives it, but that it also helps to drive. In the U.S., this system has qualities that have enabled the corporation to expand so stunningly. In particular, the laissez-faire nature of U.S. capitalism has been the most significant enabler of Amazon's relentlessness. A range of historical factors has shaped this system (also sometimes referred to as free enterprise conservatism), allowing market forces and private wealth to shape the economy and wider society, as well as reduce the influence of labour and the capacity of government to make regulatory interventions. Gibson[12] points out that: "The majority [in the U.S.] seems to recognize that laissez faire is not so much about opportunity in a fair and efficient marketplace, but is primarily about creating freedoms for a wealthy minority". Amazon has benefited extensively from this ultra-permissive form of capitalism; through it, the corporation has forced increasingly large parts of the population to rely upon it. "The Libertarian presidential candidate Harry Browne famously warned that the government will break your legs, then hand you crutches", notes Willis-Aronowitz.[13] "Mr. Browne, an ardent fan of the free market, could have been describing the economy of cheap convenience. Amazon is the clearest example of a corporation exploiting the precariousness created by capitalism – precisely by soothing some of its pain". To break away from this approach, Amazon would need to decrease its ferocious competitiveness: something that would be fundamentally at odds with its cultural profile.

52 *Lukasz Swiatek*

Having been given very wide latitude to pursue its growth, the corporation has unashamedly embraced the laissez-faire spirit of the society in which it operates to inform its actions. The corporation, unlike other digital giants, never set itself an initial high-minded ethical touchpoint to guide its operations and has simply openly pursued its commercial endeavours instead. Quinn[14] observes that:

> Whereas Google set itself up for scrutiny with its old "Don't be evil" tagline, Facebook shrouded itself in the noble cause of connecting the world, and Apple only wanted you to "think different", Amazon has never offered up any sort of ethos to the world. In that way, Amazon is . . . perhaps the greatest capitalist machine we've seen. It may obfuscate the details but it doesn't put on airs about what it's doing.

He also points out that, ironically, the corporation is one of the most beloved brands in the U.S. even though it has wreaked havoc in particular sectors. In publishing, for instance, Amazon devastated numerous booksellers, including bookstore chains that were reproached for so long about destroying much-loved local bookshops; it also caused an upheaval in the publishing industry more broadly. Its market culture means that it continues to play hardball with competitors, even being willing to undercut them where possible. Recent examples have included the announcement that third-party sellers are no longer able to use FedEx's Ground service to ship items to Prime customers; the discovery (by *The New York Times*) that Amazon Web Services borrows tools from the open-source software community, to the detriment of smaller technology companies; and the blocking of Dataxu (the ad-tech platform of the device manufacturer Roku) from ad sales for Amazon's FireTV devices, as a result of Roku and Amazon's growing competition in the streaming television devices market. These types of actions stretch back over two decades. They make it possible to "chart Amazon's 'relentless' strategy as it continues its evolution from an online store to the digital backbone of the country's infrastructure", Kovach[15] states, adding that "it's not going to stop. As Bezos likes to say, it's still 'Day One' for Amazon. And the company's relentless moves keep hurtling it forward as it grows bigger and bigger".

Amazon's ideology is embodied in numerous artefacts and practices within its symbolic universe. This type of universe consists of all of the different objectivations – that is, ideas turned into objects – that help make a particular institution in a society legitimate or valid; the symbolic universe, as an "all-embracing frame of reference" for individuals, helps explain and justify the institution through things such as specific words, sayings, legends and folktales, group rites or rituals, lore, and other traditions.[16] Individuals

Cultural Profile 53

take a particular symbolic universe for granted because it appears to be abiding or longstanding; however, such universes change because they are social products. The different purposefully built objectivations within a universe can also often act as units through which cultural memory is transmitted; this enables an organisation to shape the way in which social groups construct shared pasts.[17] Amazon has attempted to give its symbolic universe a sense of permanence by continually reproducing some of its key organisational elements.

One of the main ways in which it has given its symbolic universe fixity over time has been by continually reproducing its foundational narratives, found in one particular key objectivation: Bezos's 1997 letter to shareholders. The corporation has reprinted this letter to shareholders (from that year's annual report) in each subsequent annual report published since 1999. Every year, the 1997 letter follows the given year's letter to shareholders. The central tenets of Amazon's ideology were already evident in the 1997 letter. In the second paragraph, the founder lays out the view of the corporation's persistence and intensity, stating that:

> this is Day 1 for the Internet and, if we execute well, for Amazon.com. Today, online commerce saves customers money and precious time. Tomorrow, through personalization, online commerce will accelerate the very process of discovery. Amazon.com uses the Internet to create real value for its customers and, by doing so, hopes to create an enduring franchise, even in established and large markets.[18]

The ideology is furthered through a future-focused discourse in other parts of the letter. For instance, Bezos states that "*It's All About the Long Term*" (original emphasis),[19] "We have invested and will continue to invest aggressively to expand and leverage our customer base, brand, and infrastructure as we move to establish an enduring franchise",[20] and "We will balance our focus on growth with emphasis on long-term profitability and capital management. At this stage, we choose to prioritize growth because we believe that scale is central to achieving the potential of our business model".[21] The intensity of the corporation's focus on customers is also apparent throughout the letter. The first point in Amazon's "investment philosophy" is: "We will continue to focus relentlessly on our customers".[22] This is elaborated in the "*Obsess Over Customers*" (original emphasis)[23] section, in which Bezos notes that Amazon has brought customers:

> much more selection than was possible in a physical store (our store would now occupy 6 football fields), and presented it in a useful, easy-to-search, and easy-to-browse format in a store open 365 days a year,

54   *Lukasz Swiatek*

24 hours a day. We maintained a dogged focus on improving the shopping experience, and in 1997 substantially enhanced our store.[24]

Ironically, the remainder of the section about customers focuses not on them, but rather on transaction-related successes; it provides data about earnings from sales, orders from repeat customers, the cumulative growth in customer accounts, audience reach, and long-term relationships established with partner organisations. The remainder of the letter provides details about the organisation's infrastructure, employees, and goals for 1998.

Amazon's foundational narratives have translated, over time, into objectivations that propagate its ideology in many different places. The landing webpage of the aboutamazon.com website (connected, of course, to the main amazon.com site) outlines "Who we are"; it explains that the organisation is "guided by four principles: customer obsession rather than competitor focus, passion for invention, commitment to operational excellence, and long-term thinking".[25] These principles echo the corporation's foundational narratives, with "rather than competitor focus" being an interesting (if debatable) addition; continuity or intensity – or both – are evident in each principle as well. The organisation's mission is captured clearly on the amazon.jobs website, as well as other relevant places (such as the "Diversity and inclusion at Amazon" webpage on the aboutamazon.com site); the mission statement is another vital objectivation for the corporation and takes the following form: "Our mission is to be Earth's most customer-centric company".[26] This sort of core mission statement is vital for any organisation because it succinctly explains why the organisation exists and helps to guide the daily work of staff at various levels.[27] Despite the importance of the mission statement, at least one other mission statement has been (unhelpfully) written by Amazon, including the following statement on the "Packaging" webpage (located on the aboutamazon.com site): "Amazon's mission is to optimize the overall customer experience by collaborating with manufacturers worldwide to invent sustainable packaging that delights customers, eliminates waste, and ensures products arrive intact and undamaged".[28]

In addition to the already-mentioned key statements that help transmit its ideology, Amazon has developed a list of "Leadership Principles" that it says its staff use every day. The 14 principles are: "Customer Obsession", "Ownership", "Invent and Simplify", "Are Right, A Lot", "Learn and Be Curious", "Hire and Develop the Best", "Insist on the Highest Standards", "Think Big", "Bias for Action", "Frugality", "Earn Trust", "Dive Deep", "Have Backbone; Disagree and Commit", and "Deliver Results". Each of these principles is followed by a pithy explanation, which also conveys

Cultural Profile   55

intensity or continuity, or both. One example is the explanation for the "Insist on the Highest Standards" principle:

> Leaders have relentlessly high standards – many people may think these standards are unreasonably high. Leaders are continually raising the bar and drive their teams to deliver high quality products, services, and processes. Leaders ensure that defects do not get sent down the line and that problems are fixed so they stay fixed.[29]

These principles appear in other organisational collateral, such as Amazon's websites and its documents.

These written objectivations are, together, just one part of the corporation's symbolic universe, which also comprises a number of highly recognisable visual brand components that help sustain, and are sustained by, the ideology. The most recognisable of these elements is the brandmark, which features the word "amazon" (in lowercase letters, in a black sans-serif font) and, underneath it, a smile – represented by a curved orange line with an arrow on its right-hand side – stretching from the tail of the letter "a" to the bottom of the letter "z", which is pushed up slightly from the bottom to complete the impression of the smile. The brandmark, designed by the agency Turner Duckworth, replaced earlier logos in 2000; the iconic orange smile, connecting the letters "a" to "z", was designed to be a subtle reminder that the corporation sells everything (from A to Z, as this timeless expression goes). To further this idea, the ".com" was removed from the logo in 2012. This brandmark now appears in countless places, ranging from Amazon delivery packaging to websites. To enhance the versatility of the brandmark, Turner Duckworth also designed a "shorthand" brandmark, used on various occasions, that features content – most often the lowercase letter "a" – above the smile.[30] As the Amazon brand family grew, so did its branded house; with few exceptions, Amazon's different products and services are united through the same instantly recognisable master brand, discussed in this paragraph, that features the Amazon smile.[31] This part of the corporation's symbolic universe, its branded house, will only continue to expand as the corporation itself further rapidly expands.

Most Popular Communication and Media Offerings

Many of Amazon's most popular media and communication offerings have been integrated into the everyday lives of millions of individuals around the world. The corporation, as the opening to this chapter discussed, has not only successfully made these products and services a part of the fabric of

56 *Lukasz Swiatek*

day-to-day life; it has also made many consumers reliant on them. As this reliance increases, the organisation's logistics patterns will also increase and become even more complex, with Amazon's export patterns already having evolved significantly over the years. The organisation's "fulfilment networks" are now among the most advanced in the world, with the corporation claiming that sellers alone are able to reach 300 million customers in over 180 countries.[32]

Some of the organisation's most popular communication and media offerings are outlined in this section. Detailed sketches of every service and product are not needed; the section outlines the main features of the most popular offerings, the key benefits that they provide for consumers, and the main issue (or issues) that have been raised about them. As such, the section does not examine services and products from other areas, such as:

- Amazon Business, the purchasing solutions service for businesses;
- Amazon Cash (in the U.S.) and Amazon Top Up (in the UK), which enables customers to add a gift card automatically to their Amazon gift card balance;
- Amazon Go, the chain of convenience stores in the U.S.;
- Amazon Home Services, which enables customers to buy and schedule professional services (such as plumbing and furniture assembly) for their homes;
- Amazon Key, the delivery service that uses a specially built Amazon Lock Kit and app to allow Amazon workers to enter individuals' properties and leave their ordered packages inside; and
- AmazonFresh, the grocery delivery service.

This section also does not examine other services, products, and businesses that are controlled by Amazon (as a result of, for example, acquisition). Some of these other entities – covered in Chapter 2 of the book, in relation to Amazon's economic profile – include the following subsidiaries: Book Depository, AbeBooks, ComiXology, Fabric, IMDb and IMDbPro, Shopbop, Ring, Audible, DPReview, Woot!, CreateSpace, PillPack, ACX, the Neighbors App, Goodreads, East Dane, Zappos, Twitch (and Twitch Prime), eero, and Box Office Mojo.

Of all of Amazon's diverse media and communication offerings, it is undoubtedly the amazon.com website itself that has had the most profound impact on day-to-day life since it was launched in 1995 as an online bookstore. Over 197 million people from around the world visit the website each month.[33] Its shopping categories – including "health and household", "arts and crafts", "beauty and personal care", and "pet supplies", among many others – are deliberately designed to fulfil everyday desires. To provide further shopping opportunities, Amazon Marketplace and Amazon Second Chance have been added to the site. However, the corporation's key platform has not escaped critique. One of the loudest sets of objections made to date followed a change to the amazon.com search algorithm that boosted the corporation's own products within the search results. To instigate the change, the corporation had to overcome dissent from its own lawyers and engineers.[34]

High up on any list of Amazon's most popular products must be its Kindle reading device. Released in 2007, the device – which is designed to be a dedicated e-book reader – has continued to prove popular around the world; the corporation now promotes it as a form of comfortable entertainment, calling for the customer to "Indulge your love of reading without interruptions like email alerts and push notifications. They [Kindles] can hold thousands of books to keep you entertained for hours".[35] Kindle itself diversified into a range of other offers, including Kindle Fire (a series of tablet computers, now called Amazon Fire tablet) and Kindle Direct Publishing (a service that allows customers to self-publish e-books and paperbacks for free). The Kindle products have been critiqued over the years, though, for not having been sufficiently well built[36] and for not having provided customers with enough control over content; when the corporation remotely deleted particular e-books from the devices, warnings were sounded about a potential repeat of historical book banning.[37]

Both Alexa and the Amazon Echo device have also proven enormously popular with customers. The Alexa virtual assistant AI technology, released in 2014 and initially used on Amazon Echo "smart speakers", is designed to enhance users' everyday lives by enabling individuals to seek and receive information when they ask Alexa a question, as well as have commands executed when they give Alexa a (verbal) order. The corporation has deliberately emphasised the convenience of the products, and humanised Alexa, in its promotional collateral by stating that:

> Using Alexa is as simple as asking a question – just ask and Alexa will respond. Alexa updates through the cloud automatically and is continually learning, adding new functionality and skills. . . . Alexa can make your life easier and more fun.[38]

However, as with all AI technologies, privacy concerns have emerged since Alexa was launched. The most widespread of these concerns have related to the amount of data that the AI-enabled virtual assistant collects, and the fact that others – specifically, employees and external contractors – have listened to recorded audio clips, unbeknownst to users, in an effort to improve the service. Benjamin points out that there are broader concerns, relating

58 *Lukasz Swiatek*

particularly to the way in which the Alexa devices interact with other services. These include "the potential for putting the ears of law enforcement in our homes, schools and workplaces" and the fact that "Amazon could start tracking what health information we ask for through Alexa, effectively building profiles of users' medical histories".[39]

Film and television aficionados have long enjoyed Amazon Prime Video. Launched in the U.S. in 2006, the video-on-demand service (initially named Amazon Unbox) later had its worldwide launch in 2016. In addition to providing television shows and movies, Prime Video offers Amazon Originals: shows that are produced in-house by Amazon Studios. The service features a strategic mechanism designed to hook viewers; as Dastin explains: "Core to Amazon's strategy is the use of video to convert viewers into shoppers. Fans access Amazon's lineup by joining Prime, a club that includes two-day package delivery and other perks, for an annual fee".[40] Amazon Prime Video has been criticised for some of the entertainment choices that it has ordered or aired; a salient recent example is the 2020 television show *Hunters*, which was panned by Jewish groups for its false depictions of the Auschwitz concentration camp.[41] Further details about Amazon Prime Video can be found in the discussion of Amazon's economic profile in Chapter 2.

Closely linked to Prime Video is the Fire TV Family – which includes the Fire TV Stick, the Fire TV Cube, and the Fire TV Recast – as well as Fire Tablets. Fire TV is designed to bring live television and other streaming content from devices to larger screens; the corporation, in line with its broader discourses emphasising the importance of the consumer, promotes Fire TV by encouraging customers to "[e]asily find what to watch next with favorites and recommendations based on your viewing habits, delivered right to your home screen".[42] Fire TV Recast is an accompanying DVR (digital video recorder) that allows individuals to watch and record over-the-air television with Fire TV. On the face of it, Fire TV (and its related family of products) may seem to have been developed in order to enable customers to watch television shows and movies more conveniently; however, they actually emerged from a highly strategic commercial decision. Duhigg recounts the way in which an Amazon employee worked out the benefits of this particular set of products; the flywheel philosophy of ever-larger sales opportunities was evident in the thinking behind the products' development, as the employee mused that:

> If Amazon sold a streaming device, it could collect more data on popular shows; if Amazon had that data, it could begin profitably producing its own premium movies and television series; if Amazon made that content free for Prime members – customers who already paid ninety-nine dollars per year for two-day delivery – then more people would

sign up for Prime; if more people signed up for Prime, the company would have greater leverage in negotiating with UPS and FedEx; lower shipping costs would mean bigger profits every time Amazon sold anything on its site.[43]

The Fire TV Family has since become one of the corporation's most popular sets of products. This family, along with each of the other particularly popular media and communication products and services outlined in this section, highlights the corporation's intention of always ensuring high customer satisfaction, thus generating purchases from return shoppers, and thus fuelling increases in profits. In its development of everyday communication and media offerings, Amazon has truly been relentless.

Community Engagement

Amazon has undertaken various community engagement (and especially philanthropic) activities. Social marketing – the process that applies the principles and techniques of marketing to "create, communicate, and deliver value in order to influence target audience behaviors that benefit society as well as the target audience"[44] – has not been used as extensively by the corporation as by its competitors, for two main reasons. The first reason, discussed previously in this chapter, is Amazon's desire to blend itself quietly into the fabric of everyday life. The second reason relates to the configuration of its own marketing efforts: a configuration that deliberately supports the organisation being a sought-after ad seller (rather than being an advertiser). Amazon is increasingly approached by advertisers, due to its popularity among shoppers and its ability to deliver targeted advertising using sophisticated algorithms and an extensive amount of consumer (and other) data. Indeed, it has become so sought after[45] as an ad seller that it has recently been recognised as an "advertising giant"[46]; having climbed to the third spot in the U.S. digital advertising market (behind Google and Facebook), the corporation's ad sales are expected to rise to $28.4 billion by 2023. However, Amazon's dominance in this area, as well as its methods, have raised eyebrows. Its "frugal" approach to advertising has jarred with the longstanding approaches of the industry, while its dual role as both an e-commerce retailer and an ad seller have given it a monopolistic status; as Norman[47] explains, brand owners are conflicted because it is "clear Amazon is transferring profit and revenue from brands and retailers to itself".

Thanks to this position of strength as an ad seller, Amazon has engaged in other socially conscious promotional activities, particularly involving philanthropy. It has framed these activities around communities, saying that it focuses on "building long-term and innovative programs that will have

60 *Lukasz Swiatek*

a lasting, positive impact in communities around the world".[48] Its website promotes a raft of such community-based initiatives: for instance, the laptops it is donating to high school students ahead of at-home AP Computer Science exams, the new family shelter being constructed within its corporate office building in Seattle, and the Amazon Future Engineer robotics programme that is providing robotics grants for 100 schools. Many of these activities fall under the two salient areas on which the corporation focuses its community efforts: first, computer science and STEM education, and second, hunger, homelessness, and disaster relief.[49] These outreach efforts, overall, help Amazon in achieving the "quadruple bottom line" of corporate social responsibility (CSR) by enabling it to look after the environmental, economic, social, and cultural systems around it.[50] The organisation has also been able to display its apparent care for communities in other ways. The AmazonSmile programme uses the dedicated smile.amazon.com website to give shoppers the opportunity to have 0.5% of the price of their eligible AmazonSmile purchases donated to their chosen charitable organisation. The corporation's search for the location of its second headquarters between 2017 and 2018 provided it with the opportunity to engage in strategic issues management – that is, organisational efforts to meet, or even exceed, CSR standards[51] – by proactively tackling the different CSR-related issues that publics would be likely to raise. To that end, it listed a series of infrastructure requirements and location preferences designed to emphasise the value it placed on sustainability and the environment, community, entrepreneurship, and worker advancement; more specifically, the preferences for the second headquarters included a city with a diverse population, a stable business environment, and a demonstrable capacity for employees to enjoy living, recreational, and educational opportunities, as well as an overall high quality of life.[52,53] However, commentators, such as Postrel,[54] pointed out that the corporation was potentially conveniently using the search for the new headquarters as a way to gain handouts from local governments; she asked if the corporation wanted:

> to define itself as a scrappy competitor devoted to its customers' welfare? Or a lobbying shop looking for protection and subsidies? Does it want to sow further public cynicism, convincing the little guy that the game is rigged? Or to strengthen the rule of law? Even if all it cares about is the bottom line, the company might consider the dangerous resentment that taking the highest bid might generate from the dozens of losers.

This scrutiny of the corporation's CSR-related obligations also highlights the growing expectations that publics now have of organisations of all kinds.

Cultural Profile 61

Among Amazon's other socially conscious activities has been its support for particular causes, such as gay rights. Its founder (Bezos) and his partner set the tone in 2012; to the surprise of many observers, the couple responded to a $100,000 request for gay marriage campaign funding from the activist Jennifer Cast (one of Amazon's first employees), famously telling her: "This is right for so many reasons. We're in for $2.5 million. Jeff & MacKenzie". Bezos's focus on gay rights has filtered into Amazon practices and policies over time. For example, as part of the corporation's recent search for the location of its second set of main offices, an unspoken criterion was a city's LGBTIQA+ attitudes. As two company insiders told one reporter,[55] "[a]lthough the company's search materials don't make it explicit, Amazon has quietly made rights for and acceptance of gay and transgender people part of its criteria in choosing a second headquarters". However, the company has also been criticised for its LGBTIQA+ failures, at both the superior and subordinate levels. For instance, in 2018, shareholders demanded more diversity at the board level, leading to a requirement that women and minority candidates be considered when new board members are selected; a transgender employee in Kentucky's Amazon warehouse filed a lawsuit for workplace discrimination and pay inequality; and employees criticised the corporation's handling of ten defaced LGBT Pride posters at its headquarters.[56]

Amazon has also keenly supported sustainability efforts. Prior to 2019, the corporation's sustainability team led numerous activities designed to curb the corporation's impacts on the environment; these efforts included the construction of wind farms, the creation of partnerships with groups such as the American Council on Renewable Energy and C2ES (the Center for Climate and Energy Solutions), and the launch of an online Sustainability Question Bank.[57] In 2019, these (and other) activities were subsumed under the initiative "The Climate Pledge": a commitment, co-established with Global Optimism, for Amazon (and other signatories) to reach net zero carbon by 2040, a decade ahead of the Paris Agreement's goal of 2050. To achieve this target, the organisation is implementing or developing a range of initiatives, including redesigning packaging to reduce waste, investing in wind and solar power sources (to reach 100% renewable energy across all of its business operations by 2030), and creating a fleet of new electric vans.[58] Bezos[59] has also committed $10 billion of his own wealth to launch the Bezos Earth Fund, which will financially support scientists, activists, and non-government organisations (as well as other groups) in fighting to "preserve and protect the natural world". These major pro-environmental initiatives can, collectively, be considered a form of "corrective action" in the image-restoration efforts[60] undertaken by the corporation, following its disclosure that its 2018 carbon footprint was 44.4 million metric tonnes.[61]

62   Lukasz Swiatek

This amount, one commentator[62] has noted, amounts to approximately 85% of the annual carbon emissions of countries such as Switzerland or Denmark. Over time, all of these expanding community engagement activities will help the corporation further integrate itself into the fabric of everyday life of millions of individuals in the U.S. and around the world, just as its trade in increasingly diversified media and communication offerings (among other products and services) has done.

Notes

1. Cameron, K. S., & Quinn, R. E. (2011). *Diagnosing and changing organizational culture: Based on the competing values framework*. San Francisco: Jossey-Bass.
2. Ibid., p. 75.
3. Quinn, M. (2019, January 12). Amazon stands for nothing. That almost makes it beautiful. *Quartz*. https://qz.com/1519774/amazon-became-the-most-valuable-company-in-the-world-by-standing-for-nothing/.
4. Roberts, P. (2014). *The impulse society*. London: Bloomsbury.
5. McFadden, C. (2019, November 2). A very brief history of Amazon: The everything store. *Interesting Engineering*. https://interestingengineering.com/a-very-brief-history-of-amazon-the-everything-store.
6. Willis-Aronowitz, N. (2018, December 9). Hate Amazon? Try living without it. *The New York Times*. www.nytimes.com/2018/12/08/opinion/sunday/hate-amazon-try-living-without-it.html.
7. Fiegerman, S. (2018, April 27). Amazon made Prime indispensable – Here's how. *CNN Business*. https://money.cnn.com/2018/04/27/technology/amazon-prime-strategy/index.html.
8. Çoban, S. (2018). Introduction. In S. Çoban (Ed.), *Media, ideology and hegemony* (pp. 1–3). Leiden: Brill.
9. Gershgorn et al. (2017) op. cit.
10. Amazon: Relentless.com. (2014, June 19). *The Economist*. www.economist.com/briefing/2014/06/19/relentlesscom.
11. Stone, B. (2013). *The everything store: Jeff Bezos and the age of Amazon*. London: Bantam Press.
12. Gibson, D. (2011). *Wealth, power, and the crisis of laissez faire capitalism*. New York: Palgrave Macmillan, p. 227.
13. Willis-Aronowitz (2018) op. cit.
14. Quinn (2019, January 12) op. cit.
15. Kovach, S. (2019, December 17). The Bezos "relentless" strategy at Amazon has been on full display this week. *CNBC*. www.cnbc.com/2019/12/17/jeff-bezos-relentless-strategy-at-amazon-on-full-display.html.
16. Berger, P. L., & Luckmann, T. (1966). *The social construction of reality: A treatise in the sociology of knowledge*. New York: Doubleday, p. 89.
17. Swiatek, L. (2016). Constructing cultural memory: A memetic approach. *International Journal of Media & Cultural Politics*, 12(1), 129–142. https://doi.org/10.1386/macp.12.1.129_1.
18. Bezos, J. P. (1997). *1997 Letter to Shareholders*. Amazon, p. 1. https://ir.aboutamazon.com/files/doc_financials/annual/Shareholderletter97.pdf.

Cultural Profile 63

19. Ibid.
20. Ibid.
21. Ibid., p. 2.
22. Ibid.
23. Ibid., p. 3.
24. Ibid.
25. Amazon. (2020c). *About Amazon.com*. www.aboutamazon.com/?utm_source=gateway&utm_medium=footer.
26. Amazon. (2020d). Come build the future with us. *Amazon Jobs*. www.amazon.jobs/en/working/working-amazon/#leadership-principles.
27. Austin, E. W., & Pinkleton, B. E. (2015). *Strategic public relations management: Planning and managing effective communication programs* (3rd ed.). New York: Routledge.
28. Amazon. (2020e). Our job is making you smile. *About Amazon*. www.aboutamazon.com/sustainability/packaging.
29. Amazon. (2020f). Leadership principles. *Amazon Jobs*. www.amazon.jobs/en/principles.
30. Berman, A. (2014, August 12). A Smile is Forever on the Amazon. *Storyboard*. www.vmastoryboard.com/case-stories/2648/turner_duckworth_amazon_smile_logo/.
31. Amazon. (2020g). Images and videos. *About Amazon*. https://press.aboutamazon.com/images-videos.
32. Amazon. (2020h). The beginner's guide to selling on Amazon. *Amazon*. https://services.amazon.com.au/beginners-guide.html.
33. Dayton, E. (n.d.). Amazon statistics you should know: Opportunities to make the most of America's top online marketplace. *Big Commerce*. www.bigcommerce.com.au/blog/amazon-statistics/#executive-summary-what-this-means-for-amazon-sellers.
34. Mattioli, D. (2019, September 16). Amazon changed search algorithm in ways that boost its own products. *The Wall Street Journal*. www.wsj.com/articles/amazon-changed-search-algorithm-in-ways-that-boost-its-own-products-11568645345.
35. Amazon. (2020i). Kindle. www.amazon.com/Amazon-Kindle-Ereader-Family/b/?ie=UTF8&node=6669702011&ref_=topnav_storetab_kstore.
36. Barrett, B. (2016, April 13). Why you shouldn't spend $290 on Amazon's fancy new Kindle. *New York Magazine*. https://nymag.com/intelligencer/2016/04/why-you-shouldnt-buy-the-new-kindle-oasis.html.
37. Manjoo, F. (2009, July 20). Why 2024 will be like nineteen eighty-four. *Slate*. https://slate.com/technology/2009/07/how-amazon-s-remote-deletion-of-e-books-from-the-kindle-paves-the-way-for-book-banning-s-digital-future.html.
38. Amazon. (2020j). Meet Alexa. *Amazon*. www.amazon.com.au/b/?node=542562 2051&ref=FS_meetalexa_category.
39. Benjamin, G. (2020, January 21). Amazon Echo's privacy issues go way beyond voice recordings. *The Conversation*. https://theconversation.com/amazon-echos-privacy-issues-go-way-beyond-voice-recordings-130016.
40. Dastin, J. (2018, March 16). Exclusive: Amazon's internal numbers on Prime Video, revealed. *Reuters*. www.reuters.com/article/us-amazon-com-ratings-exclusive/exclusive-amazons-internal-numbers-on-prime-video-revealed-id USKCN1GR0FX

64 *Lukasz Swiatek*

41. Wray, M. (2020, February 24). Jewish groups criticize Amazon Prime's "Hunters" Holocaust portrayal as "foolishness". *Global News*. https://globalnews.ca/news/6588888/hunters-amazon-prime-criticism/.
42. Amazon. (2020k). Fire TV family – Amazon devices. *Amazon*. www.amazon.com/Amazon-Fire-TV-Family/b?ie=UTF8&node=8521791011.
43. Duhigg, C. (2019, October 10). Is Amazon unstoppable? *The New Yorker*. www.newyorker.com/magazine/2019/10/21/is-amazon-unstoppable.
44. Cheng, H., Kotler, P., & Lee, N. R. (2009). *Social marketing for public health: Global trends and success stories*. Sudbury, MA: Jones and Bartlett Publishers.
45. Barr, A., & Saba, J. (2018, April 24). Analysis: Sleeping ad giant Amazon finally stirs. *Reuters*. www.reuters.com/article/us-amazon-advertising/analysis-sleeping-ad-giant-amazon-finally-stirs-idUSBRE93N06E20130424.
46. O'Reilly, L., & Stevens, L. (2018, November 27). Amazon, with little fanfare,emergesasanadvertisinggiant.*TheWallStreetJournal*.www.wsj.com/articles/amazon-with-little-fanfare-emerges-as-an-advertising-giant-1543248561.
47. Ibid.
48. Amazon. (2020l). *Our communities*. www.aboutamazon.com/our-communities.
49. Ibid.
50. Schermerhorn, J. R. (2016). *Management* (6th Asia-Pacific ed.). Milton: Wiley-Blackwell.
51. Heath, R. L., & Palenchar, M. J. (2009). *Strategic issues management: Organizations and public policy challenges* (2nd ed.). Los Angeles: Sage Publications.
52. Amazon. (2017b). Amazon HQ2. *Amazon*. https://web.archive.org/web/20180118020534/www.amazon.com/b?ie=UTF8&node=17044620011.
53. Amazon. (2017c). Amazon HQ2 RFP. *Amazon*. https://web.archive.org/web/20180118172831/https://images-na.ssl-images-amazon.com/images/G/01/Anything/test/images/usa/RFP_3._V516043504_.pdf.
54. Postrel, V. (2017, October 18). Amazon has a chance to redefine corporate responsibility. *Bloomberg*. www.bloomberg.com/view/articles/2017-10-17/amazon-has-a-chance-to-redefine-corporate-responsibility.
55. O'Connell, J. (2018, April 20). The unspoken factor in Amazon's search for a new home: Jeff Bezos's support for gay rights. *The Washington Post*. www.washingtonpost.com/business/economy/the-unspoken-factor-in-amazons-search-for-a-new-home-jeff-bezoss-support-for-gay-rights/2018/04/20/9cfa8c66–31e6–11e8–8bdd-cdb33a5eef83_story.html.
56. Kim, E. (2018a, August 29). Some Amazon employees are upset at company's response to defaced LGBT office posters. *CNBC*. www.cnbc.com/2018/08/29/amazon-lgbt-posters-defaced-some-employees-upset-response.html.
57. Hurst in Murray, T. (2018, April 2). Amazon's big opportunity: Transparency in sustainability. *Forbes*. www.forbes.com/sites/edfenergyexchange/2018/04/02/amazons-big-opportunity-transparency-in-sustainability/#5d5c5c9f7c50.
58. Amazon. (2020m). Sustainability. *About Amazon*. www.aboutamazon.com/sustainability.
59. Bezos, J. [@jeffbezos] (2020, February 18). Today, I'm thrilled to announce I am launching the Bezos Earth Fund [Instagram photograph]. www.instagram.com/p/B8rWKFnnQ5c/.
60. Benoit, W. (1995). *Accounts, excuses, and apologies: A theory of image restoration strategies*. New York: State University of New York Press.
61. Amazon. (2019b). Carbon footprint. *Amazon*. https://sustainability.aboutamazon.com/carbon-footprint.
62. Marland, in Pisani, J., & Sapra, B. (2019, September 20). "Middle of the herd" no more: Amazon tackles climate change. *AP*. https://apnews.com/dd2368999232425bb5d7d2b9e84604b5.

5 Conclusion

Benedetta Brevini

The story presented in this book is the story of the extraordinary success of a corporation thriving under the current organisation of capitalism which, in absence of regulatory frameworks, favours market concentration and dominance. The expansion of Amazon was traced from its beginnings as a digital bookseller through to its morphing into a supermarket of everything and into the communications giant it is today.

A second story could be told about this growing corporation, as it is clear that Amazon's influence has extended far beyond the realm of commerce and into the realms of politics and culture. Additionally, the corporation influences the way in which we make sense of our world today. To that end, I suggest a metaphor in this final chapter that not only usefully encapsulates the way in which Amazon has evolved but also helps capture the dynamics of the organisation's power relationships with other businesses and publics.

This second story, to illustrate the proposed metaphor, begins in a kingdom not too far away. In that kingdom, a Digital Lord recently began to expand a Digital Estate. A wide variety of interesting products were available on the estate, but the lord wanted other goods to be available as well. A range of services was added to the offerings of the estate, but still this was not enough. Many diligent serfs toiled hard on the estate; however, many more were needed to increase the quantity and variety of its goods. The lord had reliable vassals, who paid rent and, in return, received services that aided their own causes. Despite their reliability, even these vassals did not satisfy the lord. An expanded estate, the lord determined, would have many more vassals. It would extend beyond the kingdom. The Digital Lord envisioned the estate covering practically the whole world, making many of the diverse and interesting goods available to people everywhere.

From afar, the Digital Lord's expansion of the estate seemed slow; behind the scenes though, it proceeded rapidly. Serfs of different kinds – some of great intellectual skill and others of great physical agility and speed – were continually brought onto the estate in ever-growing numbers. Increasing

66   Benedetta Brevini

multitudes of vassals decided to swear reverence and fealty to the lord. Ever-more wonderous products were made available on the estate, much to the excitement and delight of people near and far. So enchanting was the estate that other, smaller lords eagerly allowed themselves and their estates to be subsumed by it. *Beneficia* and loyalties became the rule. Other kingdoms also allowed the lord to sell goods from the estate. In a short time span, aspiration became reality: the Digital Lord and the estate had conquered even the furthest corners of the Earth.

The subject of the preceding fable – and the metaphor it proposes – are clear; Amazon has become one of the largest and most far-reaching corporations in the world and can be thought of as a Digital Lord with a distinctive Digital Estate. What we understand as feudalism is a significant structure of the Middle Ages. Although with many versions across European societies of the time, it is a useful metaphor to understand a series of relationships between a landowner (the lord) and their vassals and serfs with their duties, obligations, and various degrees of curtailed freedoms. As the lords of the Middle Ages extracted rents, imposed loyalties, and profited from resources that were scarce, today's Digital Lords exert their powerful dominance on their contractors, users, and citizens: us.

These Digital Lords are platforms that use their dominant position to supress competition by controlling which particular products users see and favouring their own brands over third-party suppliers. Each platform wields massive political and economic power, exerted through incremental lobbying initiatives and close ties to politics. Each platform builds a Digital Estate that is based on membership (in Amazon's case, the products as services as described in Chapter 2) and aims to lock users in. Each platform extracts rents from its third-party suppliers (vassals) who pay a fee to receive the other services of the lord, following the logic of feudal *beneficia* (in Amazon's case, Amazon Fulfilments, Amazon Advertisement, and Amazon Clouds). Thus, the sellers who do not advertise on the platform find themselves at a severe disadvantage in the market that the Digital Lord rules; like medieval vassals on an estate, loyal sellers/vassals need the lord's protection to survive. The Digital Lord is also a platform that gives users the illusion of options, but because of clear design choices and business strategies, *de facto* imposes their already-made decisions on users. The Digital Lord is also a platform that collects data about serfs and peasants in the realm (the users) through various technologies (in Amazon's case, by building its own smart homes with listening devices like Alexa). The Digital Lord is a company that exploits its financial strength, strong research capability, and market dominance to set a political agenda. The political economy of communication framework has been crucial in leading towards this metaphor that can help us understand each of today's corporate tech giants as a Digital Lord; in Amazon's case, this is explained in detail in the following sections.

Capitalising on Network Effects and Rents

Amazon has been able to exploit network effects on several levels. When Amazon started, it used its broad networks to bring in diverse suppliers, predominantly to the benefit of its customers. The more members it attracted, the more interesting it became for additional customers and the more difficult it became for alternative providers to compete. But more indirect network effects have impacted on Amazon's extraordinary success: the more consumers use Amazon, the more the platform becomes attractive not just for customers but for other indirect players in the market, third-party businesses. The more third-party retailers it attracts, the more Amazon can dictate the conditions under which they can use the platform to sell. Such conditions or fees are "rents" that progressively weaken the ecosystem of third-party sellers, establishing a more repressive Digital Estate that gives retailers no other choice but to accept the condition of the lord. Moreover, Amazon does not compete only with major e-shopping companies offering platforms for retailers: it also competes with the same sellers as a producer that sells its products in the same ecosystem. This is unfair competition, as the Digital Lord does not pay rents to sell its own products.

Reinforcing Its Concentrated Economic and Political Power

As one of the Digital Lords with dominant market power, Amazon uses its assertive position to restrain competition by controlling which products users see in their realm and by promoting its own brands. Meanwhile, Amazon's advertising business is also thriving, so retailers are also forced to pay additional rent to advertise on the platform. This uncontested dominance allows a Digital Lord like Amazon to push a mechanism of loyalty and *beneficia* to the company (for both vassals and serfs) to keep all users, providers, and retailers permanently attached to its services. This is through the creation of a proprietary system environment, enriched by the incredible technological assets of the company (AWS for example), that offers customised and integrated hardware products, services that are designed to keep vassals and serfs within the same estate forever.

Another factor is crucial in pushing the concentration dynamics and the consolidation of market power of Amazon: its impressive financial resources in the form of stock market capital that enables continuous acquisition and the elimination of potential competitors. The Digital Estate's

68 *Benedetta Brevini*

ever-expanding capital has been fuelled by the flywheel philosophy of its founder: a philosophy that entails a continuous process of prices being lowered to attract more customers and increase sales, allowing the estate to lower its operating costs in order to cut prices again, thus keeping the flywheel perpetually spinning. The Digital Lord's substantial capital enables continuous expansion into new territories; lord and estate have continued to sweep across new lands and conquer other, smaller lords and estates, bringing their serfs (workers) and vassals (third parties) under its aegis. The lord's growing capital also enables expansion through experimentation; serfs are encouraged to develop new goods that the estate will be able to sell to new subjects.

The modern expansionist Digital Estate requires different mechanisms to grow in comparison with the estates of old, and Amazon has certainly made use of these mechanisms to increase its political influence. It has engaged in increasingly sophisticated lobbying activities. The court of the lord has expanded in recent years to include a number of expert lobbyists, drawn from the ranks of the political-corporate elite, who have been undertaking activities to try to persuade lawmakers (and other parties) of the worthiness of the corporation's actions. This part of the lord's court has used ever-greater precision and intensity in its activities thanks to the digital tools at its disposal. This has been particularly important during the reign of a king (Donald Trump) who has been unhappy with the lord's rapid expansion of the estate, threatening the king's own interests and activities.

Data Extraction as Core Business

Amazon's business strategies, like the business strategies of other Digital Lords, have always been characterised by an obsession for data extraction and profile building. Thus, Amazon as a Digital Lord has systematically collected, matched, and evaluated users' behaviour on its platform and beyond to create an impressive database of profiles. These large volumes of data are used to create ever-more differentiated user profiles, which are employed to anticipate what users want. But this data is also fundamental to feed a number of other businesses of the Digital Lord; they are used to develop the most successful products sold under the Amazon brands, crucially tied to consumers' preferences (to reiterate their status of vassals, third-party sellers on Amazon don't have access to their own customers' data). These profiles serve as an important input for its research and development, and they feed all Artificial Intelligence expansions and Internet of Things products.[1] Ultimately, they also contribute to their growing advertising activities, ultimately aimed at influencing users' behaviour and actions.

Making the Digital Estate Attractive

In order to make the growing estate attractive to a range of individuals and groups – including new serfs and vassals who have been conquered, and prospective new serfs and vassals who continue to be attracted – any Digital Lord has to employ an array of tools from marketing and public relations (among other areas). Amazon has extensively focused on philanthropic and community-based social engagement efforts, particularly in these areas: hunger, homelessness, and disaster relief, as well as computer science and STEM education. Its website contains a treasury of case studies detailing the different individuals and groups who have been assisted by these efforts. As the corporation has become one of the largest ad sellers in America (and the world), with a sophisticated advertising system that uses advanced digital algorithms to match goods with consumers' searches and past purchases, it does not need to engage in other forms of social marketing. As the world's priorities shift in the face of unrest from populist politics and the climate crisis (among other pressing grand challenges), Amazon has also become attuned to the importance of corporate social responsibility; it has made increasing efforts to show that it cares about the environmental, economic, social, and cultural systems around it.

A sophisticated symbolic universe has also been built for Amazon over time that has enabled it to advance its ideology of continuous, intense action. Articulated initially by Bezos, the organisation's corporate mantra – of being the world's most customer-centric business – has been pushed in all areas of activities. It has also taken physical form through items such as letters to shareholders and other corporate documents, written and audio/visual content on the Amazon website and its connected sites, and leadership principles, among many others. These messages have also been shared through the organisation's many popular products and services – ranging from the Kindle to Alexa – part of everyday life for millions of individuals. The Amazon brand family, anchored in the highly recognisable brandmark (featuring the distinctive orange Amazon smile), has been another major component in promoting the ideology and nurturing the corporation's accelerated growth. As every Lord in medieval times relied on a powerful religious ethos to secure their domains, the enormously successful advertising operations of Amazon could be seen as an example of spiritualism at work.

The Future of the Digital Lord

The past may hold some clues about the future of Amazon and other Digital Lords. Indeed, it is helpful to return right back to the feudal past in order

70 Benedetta Brevini

to advance into a potential future. Etymologically, the word 'lord' can be traced back to the Old English *hlāford*, which originated from *hlāfweard*, meaning 'loaf-ward' or 'bread keeper', reflecting the Germanic tribal custom of chieftains providing food for their followers.[2] Amazon will, no doubt, continue to be a provider for its followers: a provider of a growing number of products, as well as an increasing array of services.

However, just as the feudal system of nobility in the past met a gradual end with the rise of enlightened thinking and the shift to democratic societies, so too may Amazon and other Digital Lords gradually meet a similar fate. Already, in recent years, the critical eye of lawmakers has been turning increasingly to Amazon; in the U.S. in particular, concerted efforts have begun to be made to rein in the largest corporate (tech) giants. Individuals and groups – ranging from the civil society activists of non-government organisations to smaller businesses – have gradually realised that Digital Estates contain multiple (and growing) traps beyond their glittering, beautiful facades. Although Amazon is unlikely to be toppled from its lordly position, pushback against it is likely to grow in the coming years.

Notes

1. For example, see Brevini, B. (2020). Creating the technological saviour: The myth of artificial intelligence in Europe. In P. Verdigen (Ed.), *AI for everyone?* London: University of Westminster Press.
2. Oxford Dictionary of English.

Index

AbeBooks 15, 56
acquisition 14, 18, 31, 36, 67
advertising 9–18, 36, 59, 67
Alexa 12–16
Alibaba 19
Alphabet 7, 18, 34
Amazon: founding of 8–10;
  marketplace 9–17, 51, 57; markets of
  13–19, 53; ownership of 11–16
Amazon Advertising 18
Amazon Business 56
Amazon Cash 56
Amazon Fresh 36
Amazon Go 56
Amazon Home Services 56
Amazon Key 56
Amazon Marketplace 9, 10, 57
Amazon Prime *see* Prime
Amazon Robotics 41, 14
Apple (company) 7, 14–15, 34, 36, 52
Artificial Intelligence (AI) 14–15, 68;
  see also Alexa
Audible 14–20
AWS 7–15; *see also* cloud services

behavior 30, 39, 68
Bezos, J. 1–2, 12–13, 22–40; Bezos Act
  39; biography of 22
Board of Directors (Amazon) 24–26
Book Depository 15, 56
brand 7, 17, 52–59
business divisions 10
business strategies 5, 66, 68

capitalism: big data 4; platform 4;
  super 2; surveillance 4
China 19

cloud services 4, 7, 9, 13–15; *see also*
  AWS
Communication Giant 3, 5, 6, 7, 9;
  see also digital, Giant
computer 14, 57, 60, 69
concentration 3, 65–67
consolidated statements 9
consumer 1, 4, 12–23, 28–35
contractors 57–66
corporate governance 22–24
corporation 1–5, 14
COVID-19 1, 41, 46
cultural profile 48–51

data: big 4; extraction 4–5, 18, 30; use
  of 3–6
datafication 42
digital: Giant 13, 31, 34, 36, 52; Lord
  3, 5, 65–66; products 14
diversification 7, 48
dominance 16, 18, 19, 24, 59, 65–67

e-commerce 17, 19, 59
economic: development 33; profile 7–11
Estate, Digital 65–70
European 5, 62
everyday life 48, 49, 55–62

Facebook 4, 7, 18, 31, 34, 52, 59
fee 4, 9, 11, 13, 17, 38, 49, 51
feudalism 58, 66
financial crisis 2, 58
financial resources 67
Forbes 7, 22, 42

games 14, 16, 17
Gandy, O. 4, 6

72 Index

Gates, B. 6, 25, 27
global giant 3
Google 7, 17, 18, 31, 32, 34
Greenspan, A. 34, 36

Hayek, P. 3
hour, salary per 28, 38, 40, 41
human resources 27
human *vs.* robots 14, 57

ideology 5, 27, 48, 50–62, 69
IMDb 16, 56
immigration 29, 33
income 8–10
influence 3, 7, 19, 22, 31, 34, 35, 36,
     51, 59, 65, 68
information 10, 25, 29, 32, 57, 58
Internet 3–5, 13, 16
Internet of Things 4, 68
investment 5, 9, 18, 23, 24, 30, 41, 43, 53

jobs 2, 14, 26, 30, 36; controversies
     37–41

Katz, M. L. 3, 6
Kindle 14–16, 57, 69
Kiva 14, 41
Kovach, S. 52
Kushner, J. 25

labour 19, 22, 37–41
law, rule of 60, 68
lawsuit 27–29, 61
leadership, principles 54, 69
lobbying 24–35
Lord, Digital 5, 65–70

Mazzucato, M. 4
McChesney, R. 4
media 9, 13, 15–17, 25
Microsoft 7, 14, 15, 17, 34, 37
mobile 14, 15, 41
monopoly 4
Mosco, V. 4
Murdock, G. 8
music 13–16, 36

narratives 53–54
Netflix 2
net sales 9–11

network 11, 15, 18, 25, 26, 36, 56
network effect 3–5, 67
New York Stock Exchange 1
New York Times 17, 38

Obama, B. 28, 30–32
online advertising 9, 11, 67–69;
     revenue of 11, 13, 18
online stores 11
operating income 10, 53
organization 22–28
organizational culture 32, 39, 48
ownership 3–5, 16, 22–26

platform 4, 12–19, 42, 52, 57, 66–68
policy 5, 31–40
political agenda 22, 26, 66
political economy of communication 2, 3
political profile 5, 22–25
popular 48, 49, 55–69
power 18, 19, 22, 23, 34, 36
Prime 2, 9, 13–18, 37, 50, 52, 56
Prime Day 18
privacy 29–31, 36, 57
public 1–5, 8, 16
public relations 32, 39, 69
publics 39, 50, 60, 65

rent 3–5, 7–9, 65–69
reports 5, 9, 11, 18
research and development 14, 68
robotics 14, 41, 60; *see also* Amazon
     Robotics

Sanders, B. 2, 39–40
scarce resources 5, 66
Securities and Exchange Commission
     (SEC) 5, 9, 22
security 13–15, 29, 33
Shapiro, C. 3
shipping 9, 13–19, 37, 50, 59
shock doctrine 2
Srnicek, N. 4
stores 11, 13, 56
subscription 9, 11, 13–18
success 4, 5, 7, 9, 10, 14, 18, 27, 31, 33,
     37, 40, 48
supermarket 17, 65
sustainability 54, 60, 61
symbolic 5, 48, 50, 52, 55

Index 73

technology 3, 9, 12, 13, 21, 23–42
third party sellers 4–19, 52, 56
trade group 5, 19, 32, 40, 42
Trump, D. 25, 27, 28, 32, 35, 36, 37, 40
Twitch 14, 17, 56
Twitter 34, 39
"two pizza rule" 13

value 3, 4, 18; real 53
vassal 65–69

venture capital firm 25
vertical merger 33

warehouse 1, 5, 8, 14, 19, 38, 40–41
wealth 1, 3, 22, 51, 61
web 51, 52, 54–56
white collar 38, 41, 48
Whole Foods 17–18, 36
Withoutabox 16
women 17, 37, 61
workers 1, 2, 28, 34, 38–40

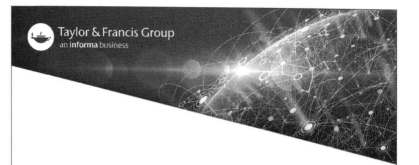